THE POCKET CRYSTAL CHAKRA HEALER

PHILIP PERMUTT

The best-selling author of *The Crystal Healer*

CICO BOOKS

This hardback edition published in 2026
by CICO Books
An imprint of Ryland Peters & Small Ltd
20–21 Jockey's Fields, London WC1R 4BW
1452 Davis Bugg Road, Warrenton,
NC 27589
www.rylandpeters.com
Email: euregulations@rylandpeters.com

First published in 2009 as *The Complete Guide to Crystal Chakra Healing*

10 9 8 7 6 5 4 3 2 1

A CIP record for this book is available from the British Library.
US Library of Congress CIP data has been applied for.

ISBN: 978-1-80065-582-9

Printed in China

Photography: Geoff Dann and Roy Palmer
Illustrators: Tiffany Lynch and Trina Dalziel

Senior designer: Emily Breen
Art director: Sally Powell
Creative director: Leslie Harrington
Production manager: Gordana Simakovic
Publishing manager: Carmel Edmonds

The authorised representative in the EEA is
Authorised Rep Compliance Ltd.,
Ground Floor. 71 Lower Baggot Street,
Dublin, D01 P593, Ireland
www.arccompliance.com

SAFETY NOTE

Please note that while the descriptions of the properties of crystals refer to healing benefits, they are not intended to replace diagnosis of illness or ailments, or healing or medicine. Always consult your doctor or other health professional in the case of illness.

MIX
Paper | Supporting responsible forestry
FSC® C106563

CONTENTS

FOREWORD

***The Complete Guide to Crystal Chakra Healing* was originally published in 2009, at a time when holistic practices were being challenged more and more by the allopathic medical community.**

What these people failed to understand is that although surgery and drug intervention can help critical conditions, they do nothing to address the concept of bodymind (see page 7), which is where all chronic conditions are seated, where the whole being is affected by dis-ease. In fact, in my experience, all cases of illness have their cause not in the physical body but in the bodymind.

Take, for example, one of my clients who went to hospital with a broken leg because she was run over by a bus. The hospital set the bone and put the leg in a cast, then tidied up the cuts and grazes and sent her on her way. Around nine months later, when this person's leg was fully healed, she was run over by a car. She came to me thinking she'd been cursed. However, after just one treatment it became apparent that she had a lot of stress at work and issues about changing careers and moving forward. She was distracted by this stress every day for most of the day. This is why she was so preoccupied that she didn't even see the huge bus that knocked her over. Over a series of crystal chakra healing treatments, she became less stressed and could make the decisions about changes she needed to make in her life—and to the best of my knowledge, she has never been knocked down by a car again since. Her being knocked down by vehicles was never the dis-ease, but a symptom of her chronic problem.

Recent developments in science have suggested that the way mystics have seen the world for the past millennia may indeed be correct. There are two universes of energy within our world: the physical, which we can all see and touch, and that which science calls *dark matter* and *dark energy*, which is invisible to most people but is starting to explain the mystic world. It has been proved that the two exist together and intermingle, and the dark energy affects the physical world we see. Crystals work on the level of the bodymind. They do not work on the physical body, but their energy influences us on subtle levels, bringing changes to our physical being; by healing our chakras and energy system, the crystals bring physical healing, too.

I put together *The Complete Guide to Crystal Chakra Healing* to enable readers to utilize those healing energies, filling the book with the knowledge I've spent years building up—how crystals focus, store, transmit, and transmute energy, how our internal chakra systems function, and how to perform full crystal chakra healing treatments. This pocket-sized edition presents you with all of the valuable information in a format that you can enjoy on the go and refer back to again and again. My hope is that with this book, even more people will enjoy the healing benefits that crystals can bring.

Philip Permutt

INTRODUCTION

This book contains information from my own personal journey with crystals—or the Stone People, as they are sometimes called—working on myself and with customers, clients, and students almost every day for nearly 35 years.

My experiences have given me a practical understanding of the body's energy system and shown me how crystals and their healing powers interact with the chakras, aura, and meridians to bring about positive changes in people's lives. It is this knowledge that is brought to you in this book. Some of the information comes directly from my clients and students, while other facts come from research into ancient and contemporary writings. Where I have drawn upon these, I have, whenever possible, tested the information either on myself or on my willing students.

I'm often asked whether I believe crystals work. The answer is no… I know they work. One client even said that he didn't think the crystal chakra healing treatments he was about to embark on would work, and did he have to believe in crystals for them to work? You don't have to believe in crystals for them to work just as you don't have to believe that the light will come on when you turn on the light switch. Nor do you have to believe that the chakras of your energy system exist for you to wake up in the morning and breathe. Of course, like all other types of treatment (including medical), there is a placebo effect, but, as you will see, this is not all there is to it. People have been working successfully with crystals and applying them to chakra healing all around the world for thousands of years.

Crystal colors are created by other mineral inclusions, optical discrepancies in the crystalline structure or processes such as heat and radiation. Clockwise from top: polished quartz crystal, aqua aura, citrine, imperial topaz, amethyst, natural quartz crystal, and polished citrine.

Skeptics will always cite reasons why crystals can't work. These are usually based on the undisputed fact that there is no scientific proof of crystals curing any specific illness. Nevertheless, the answer to that is simple—try it yourself. As I'll explain, the "bodymind," or your body's energy system, which links mind, body, and spirit, doesn't have specific illnesses but is interlaced with moving, vibrant, constantly changing energy. When you experience personally the effects of crystal healing through your chakras on your own energy system, you know for certain that something positive is happening.

As you turn the pages of this book, you'll find many practical exercises. Please do try them. It is only through working with crystals that you can begin to understand them. You can use this book as a workbook, reading from start to finish, or dip in and out of the crystal and chakra information and the healing techniques as you see fit.

You will be introduced to crystals and the body's energy system—the chakras, aura, and meridians—and learn through the method of crystal chakra healing how to select and cleanse crystals and then apply them for self-healing, healing others, and changing your environment. Just bringing the natural beauty of crystals into your home will change how you feel—they make you feel good. They are safe to work with and have no unhelpful side effects because if you, or more precisely the energies within you, are already balanced, then your crystal will have to do nothing more than simply look pretty.

Whether this is the start of your journey with crystals and energy, or another step on a well-trodden path, open your heart and mind and allow yourself to feel the energy of possibility flow through you.

A polished amethyst, showing concentric rings formed during the crystal's growth.

Mixed varieties of jasper and rhyolite.

CHAPTER 1

INTRODUCING CRYSTAL CHAKRA HEALING

Welcome to the start of your journey into crystal chakra healing. Chakras and crystals are intrinsically linked through their connections with energy—the chakras are the doorways through which the positve healing energies of crystals can enter the body. By following the expert advice in this book, you will begin an enlightening journey focusing on the relationships between crystals and chakras that will help you to achieve a healthy body, mind, and spirit.

UNDERSTANDING CHAKRAS

Placing crystals directly on and around your chakras, or energy centers, creates an internal energy balance that leads to healing and improved well-being. Chakras draw the healing energies of the crystals into your body and then release this power through the meridians, or energy pathways, and out into your surrounding aura.

Crystals have their own unique energies that balance your energies. You can effect beneficial changes to your body, mind, spirit, and emotions by applying crystals using both ancient and modern healing techniques, including:

- Wearing or carrying crystals (pages 31–33)
- Laying on of stones (pages 33–34)
- Preparing crystal elixirs (pages 35–37)
- Rotating crystals to focus energy (pages 12, 188)
- Crystal chakra healing (pages 175–197)

Each chakra has associated healing crystals. These are the chakra "set" of seven, for each of the seven chakras (see pages 53 and 57).

DOORWAYS TO ENERGY EXCHANGE

Chakras are the key to the crystal chakra healing method described fully in this book. By drawing in, processing, and distributing life force energy (also known as *chi* or *prana*), chakras act as the doorways to the healing energies of crystals. There are seven major chakras, which control the health of specific areas of your body as well as the way you interact with the external energy of other people, your surroundings, and your lifestyle.

This interaction of energy underpins many alternative-medicine healing systems, including Ayurvedic medicine (AM) and traditional Chinese medicine (TCM). The chakras tie in with acupuncture points and also relate to the key energy storage centers in Taoist healing. First systematized in ancient India, chakras form part of the underlying belief systems of religions such as Hinduism and Buddhism, and spiritual energy practices such as Reiki healing and yoga. They fit within systems that link the body and mind into one indivisible unit, sometimes known as the bodymind.

In some Eastern thought, the chakras are seen as levels of consciousness linked with the soul, which relates to different areas of physical life: the physical body, instinct, vital energy, emotion, communication, the overview of life, and connection to the divine. The chakras are arranged within the body like a ladder for the soul to climb, from matter (the crude form of consciousness) at the base to pure consciousness at the crown.

People who can see energy often describe chakras as spinning spheres or wheels—"chakra" is derived from the Sanskrit *chakrum*, meaning circle or wheel. There isn't a vocabulary for subtle-energy phenomena, so each person describes the experience in their own way, as they perceive it. The same is true of crystal healing energies.

PRACTICAL EXERCISE: Sensing Energy

Practicing this exercise will help you sense the energy inside and around you in response to the interplay between a crystal and your body's energy system. Take note of these feelings, as they are sometimes very subtle. However you describe crystal energy will be unique to you. Don't worry about what you feel or where you feel it—only that you feel something. If you have a journal or notebook, it can be helpful to record your experiences.

- Find a quiet space in which you will not be disturbed. Then, with a friend present, close your eyes and hold both of your hands out flat in front of you, with your palms up.
- Ask your friend to hold a quartz crystal over the palm of one of your hands, with the termination pointing toward your palm. Now ask your friend to rotate the quartz crystal slowly 1–2 in/2.5–5 cm above one of your palms.
- Notice the difference in how your two hands feel. Look for physical feelings, such as one hand being warmer, cooler, heavier, lighter, itchier, and so on. Don't worry too much about what you feel, where you feel it, or how you describe it—the important thing is that you feel a difference, however slight, between the hand with the quartz crystal above it and the other hand. If you don't sense anything, try shaking your hands vigorously before you begin—this seems to make it easier to sense subtle energy.

UNDERSTANDING CRYSTALS

Crystals are naturally occurring solids made from minerals. Most are formed in the earth's surface; some are formed by inorganic processes, such as sedimentation, while others, such as moldavite, are born in the stars. Residing in the heavens, they fall to earth as meteors.

In scientific terms, a crystal is a solid form of a mineral or other substance. Coming in all shapes, sizes and colors, each type of crystal has a precise atomic arrangement and mineral composition, making it unique. They can be identified by their crystal form, color (although colors can vary, not only within one type of crystal but also individual specimens of the same crystal), specific gravity, and their degree of hardness as measured by the Mohs Scale of Mineral Hardness. The Mohs Scale is named after Friedrich Mohs, a German inventor, who discovered the constant relationship of how hard minerals are in relation to one another.

Natural dioptase

Blue lace agate

Fire agate

NATURAL CRYSTAL SHAPES

Amethyst

Each type of crystal is formed by a specific group of atoms, in a fixed structure, creating a unit cell. These cells are stacked in a precise three-dimensional pattern that is described as the crystal system. Crystals can be grouped depending on their crystal system. A defining property of a crystal is its inherent symmetry, which is dependent on the crystal system of its structure.

Angelite

There are seven crystal systems that define the natural shape of any specific crystal. These are: cubic, hexagonal, tetragonal, rhombohedral, orthorhombic, monoclinic, and triclinic. So, for example a cubic crystal, such as pyrite, will always have the symmetry of a cube, whereas a hexagonal crystal, like quartz, will always have six sides.

Aqua aura

Crystals can also be cut and polished into any shape. Common polished shapes are the point or obelisk, sphere, egg, heart, angel, faceted stone, and tumble stone. Tumble stones are tumbled with grits in barrels, to smooth and polish them, and are the most widely available form of many crystals.

Pink rhodochrosite

A NOTE ON TERMINOLOGY Throughout this book, the term "crystal" is not limited to the scientific definition but also includes all of the mineral kingdom, the Stone People, crystals, minerals, rocks, stones, and gemstones.

EXPLORING THE POWER OF CRYSTALS

Crystals are scattered throughout the literature of the ages, including ancient Chinese writings on traditional medicine and India's Ayurvedic texts. The Bible has over 200 references to crystals and their powers and associations, while the text *Peri Lithon* ("On Stones") by the ancient Greek philosopher Theophrastus is the basis of today's modern scientific classification of gemstones. His taxonomy of known gems describes their origin, physical properties, and magical and healing powers. Crystals have also been found around the world in the graves of ancient cultures, including Ancient Egypt and the Olmec civilization of South America.

Mankind has been aware of the power of crystals for thousands of years—yet science has yet to explain exactly how and why they work. We know that they focus, transmit, transmute, and store energy. Like everything in the universe, they vibrate. Some can produce electrical effects, namely the piezoelectric effect (in response to mechanical stress) and the pyroelectric effect (in response to being heated). Crystals increase the frequency of light and affect the movement of photons of light. They "learn" things and communicate information in much the same way as radio signals, evolving their healing capabilities to suit changes in their environment. Scientists have been intrigued for many years by the theory that crystals have the ability to act as primitive genes, and research into the "crystals-as-genes" theory is pioneering our knowledge of crystal inheritance mechanisms.

Rough manganoan calcite and polished erythrite.

PRACTICAL EXERCISE:

Sensing Crystal Energy in the Heart Chakra

- Hold a quartz crystal 1–2 in/2.5–5 cm from the center of your chest (this is your heart chakra; see also page 108). Now begin to move it slowly in counterclockwise circles.
- It may take a few minutes, but you will notice something—not just in your hand or the crystal or over your chest, but within you. You may feel happy or elated, sad, or emotional. You may give your feeling many words (you are creating a vocabulary) but you will feel "something." It is essentially energy flowing in, through, and out of your heart chakra: balancing, healing, and creating the possibility for change.

Western science has shown the existence of the body's energy system in terms of the aura and chakras; the meridians have been mapped by Japanese doctors. At present, the only way we can understand the bodymind and its associated energy is through experience. Dr. Hiroshi Motoyama, Head of the Institute for Life Physics in Tokyo and the California Institute for Human Science, has developed two machines—one that can measure life force energy and the other the energy of the chakras. He says, "That is how we can find this mechanism for the interaction between the mind and the body. That is a new science, or not a new science perhaps but a new medicine... So now we are just approaching this door to open." To sense crystal energy in your own energy system, try the exercise opposite.

CRYSTAL CHAKRA HEALING FOR ANIMALS

I was recently asked whether animals have chakras. Yes, everything from ants upward on the evolutionary scale has seven chakras. This fact may be linked to the segmentation of the body (clearly seen in insects) and Hock's genes (on human chromosome 12), which act as master switches, controlling the activity of genes and how they interact with one another. Very early in the development of the fetus, they help the identical cells formed during its early growth to differentiate and form the various segments of the body, and later the specific organs, limbs, etc, residing in each region of the adult body. As this process of development is essentially the same for almost all animals, it is logical to assume that animals' energy systems are also fundamentally the same, developing along the same segmented path. Both my experience and many others' experience of healing domestic and farm animals bear this out.

Working with my own dogs over the years, I have found that crystals have very similar effects on them as on me or any human subject. You can apply crystal chakra healing to pets and livestock yourself, but you will need some understanding of your pets or you can simply dowse crystals with your pendulum (see pages 23–24). Attach the selected crystals to collars, place them in beds and water bowls (but note that some crystals are not safe to place in water—see page 35), and put them in or tie them to cages.

However you choose to work with crystals, learning to control the flow of life-force energy allows you to make positive alterations to your health and lifestyle. This book is a handbook to health, containing many techniques for working with crystals on the chakras, aura, and meridians of the body's energy system. You can use it to improve the quality of your life and that of your clients, healing mind, body, and spirit.

Attaching crystals to animals' collars helps them benefit from the crystal's healing energies.

CHAPTER 2

WORKING WITH CRYSTALS

From choosing crystals that are right for you to making therapeutic crystal elixirs, crystals can become part of your everyday experience. This chapter explores how to work with crystals, such as dowsing with a crystal pendulum and crystals for meditation, to help your journey along the healing path.

SELECTING CRYSTALS

There are three simple ways to select the crystals you need, whether for yourself or for others:

- Look them up in a book such as this one (see Chapter 4). Decide why you need a crystal and search for the appropriate ones to help the condition or symptoms.
- Follow your intuition. Feeling drawn in any way to a crystal suggests that you need it. It will stand out from the crowd, possibly sparkle and shine, and virtually shout at you, wave, jump up and down, or leap off the shelf. Of course, it may just be interesting or look pretty. However you are drawn to them, these crystals will help you, sometimes in unexpected or amazing ways. If you are selecting crystals for other people, perhaps as a gift, then keep that person in your mind when choosing. Sometimes it's helpful to look at a photograph of the person, have a personal object that belongs to them, or even just write their name on a piece of paper.
- Employ a pendulum and dowse for the crystals you need (see pages 23–24).

If you are selecting crystals intuitively or with a pendulum, you can always look up their healing properties in a book. Conversely, if you have chosen crystals from a book, you can decide how best to apply them with the aid of a pendulum. The most important thing when choosing a crystal is to trust yourself.

CRYSTALS YOU DON'T LIKE

When I talk about crystals you "notice" or are "drawn to," that includes those crystals you don't like, too. In fact, these are the ones that will really help on the deepest level. Things happen to all of us throughout our lives; some are wonderful but others unpleasant. Most of the uncomfortable experiences you have, you face and deal with in one way or another. However, every now and then, perhaps for no obvious reason, you suppress your feelings. If something starts to trigger these hidden emotions, you suppress them again, burying them ever deeper and avoiding any reminder of the situation that created them. You've avoided awaking this repressed emotion for so long that you probably don't even know you're doing it or what the issue was in the first place. Now it's buried deep in your subconscious—and the crystals that you don't like are going to bring it to the surface. When you work with these crystals, you will feel emotional, perhaps shedding some tears or being irritable, as you release the ensnared disturbing experience. Sometimes the process can be rough, but it won't last long, and after you free the emotion, you'll feel better. You will never have to avoid something again because of this repressed emotion—even if you hadn't realized what it was in the first place.

These are all varieties of calcite.

PREDICTIVE CRYSTALS

Crystals can be predictive: you may be drawn to one you will need in the near future. It happens regularly in my shop where someone chooses crystals or I've dowsed for them with my pendulum. Turquoise came up for a customer recently and I just knew it was to do with travel. She denied she had any travel plans but took the crystal anyway, as she'd been drawn to it. A couple of days later she came in again, astonished that she'd had an unexpected promotion at work and would have to spend a few days each week in the company's New York office.

When you select crystals for yourself, you may also be drawn to crystals for other people you are thinking about. Clients and friends are drawn to you because of who you are and your own unique energy, so don't be surprised if the same or similar crystals and issues keep coming up.

Abalone shell

Hemimorphite

PENDULUM DOWSING

Dowsing is a natural and ancient human ability, possibly the oldest form of divination. We know that people have been dowsing since before recorded time, as the earliest writings talk of dowsing in a matter-of-fact way. Today dowsing is used by therapists in many fields, as well as by water and oil companies throughout the world. It can be done with a pendulum, rod, or forked twig, but a pendulum is the most portable and straightforward to work with when dowsing over a client.

Choosing and Working With a Pendulum

A pendulum gives you a physical representation of your natural inner knowing. It consists of a piece of metal, wood, or crystal hanging on a chain or string. A crystal pendulum requires less effort to work with when you start, as crystals magnify energy, which makes tuning into them simpler and their answers more obvious. When you choose your pendulum, don't think about it too much—simply stand in front of a selection and pick the first one you notice. As with choosing crystals, you need to trust your instincts.

Dowse over your crystals with a pendulum to select them for healing work.

PRACTICAL EXERCISE:
Asking the Pendulum Questions

- Before you can ask the pendulum questions, you need to know how to recognize "yes" and "no." Hold it in your hand and ask a simple question for which you know the answer is yes, such as, "Am I a woman/man?" The pendulum will start to make a movement such as swinging back and forth, side to side, or in circles. This is your pendulum's "yes" response.
- Now ask the opposite question and you should see a different movement. You have identified the pendulum's "no" response.
- To use the pendulum to select crystals, simply hold it over a number of crystals one at a time, ask, "Do I need this crystal?" and watch for the "yes" or "no" response.
- You can ask the pendulum any question you wish. However, as with all spiritual tools, pendulums respond to how they are treated. If you are serious and phrase your questions sensibly, so that they can be answered in the affirmative or negative, your pendulum will always give you the correct answer. But if you treat it as a game or continually ask the same question over and over, it will respond accordingly.

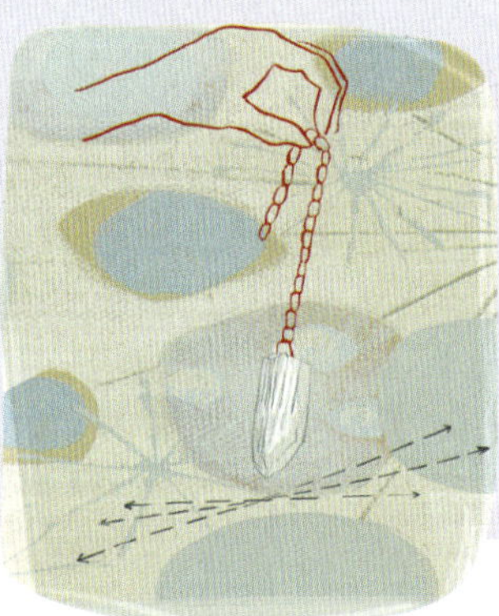

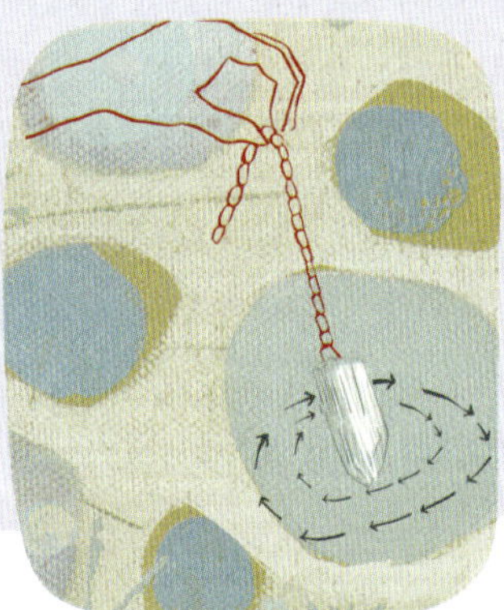

The Internal Pendulum

We have two distinct reactions to everything that happens to us. We react with a feeling of "yes" or "no," exactly as a pendulum does, which is why we can see this as our internal pendulum. Most people only recognize these reactions in extreme situations involving danger, dread, excitement, or joy.

- In times of extreme fear we get a sinking feeling that starts in the solar plexus and sinks into the gut. This "inner no" is saying, "Don't do it," or "I don't want to be here—I should go."
- The opposite of this is the "inner yes," accompanying joy or excitement. It's an uplifting feeling, rising from the solar plexus to the heart. It says, "Wow, this is fantastic," "I love this," "I'm having fun," or "This is the right thing to be doing."

The feelings of fear and excitement are often confused, as they are both extremes emanating from the same point, and most exciting things are usually a little scary, too. However, they are actually opposites.

Amethyst, quartz, and rose quartz are popular pendulum crystals.

The more attention you pay to this internal pendulum, the more you will notice it. In fact, these reactions happen on a very small scale in connection with everyone we meet and everything we do, see, and hear. As you work more with your crystal pendulum, you'll start to notice that the crystal pendulum says "yes" when you are feeling slightly uplifted, and it says "no" when you are feeling slightly down. Gradually you will become more aware of your internal pendulum, with the result that, in time, you need to rely less on your crystal pendulum.

Many pendulums have regular facets; others may be natural.

CLEANSING CRYSTALS

You can see when a crystal needs cleansing—it loses its sparkle, brightness, and even color, and may feel sticky in your hand. Dust is drawn to crystals because of their electric properties, adhering to them through an electrostatic charge. This alters their natural healing abilities, reducing the number of photons of light reaching the crystal. Regular cleansing prevents a buildup of dust.

The other reason crystals have to be cleansed is that they pick up energy when we are working with them, either from ourselves or from others. They will even pick up energy from people in a shop and, in fact, may have been handled by many customers before you. There is nothing wrong with these energies—they're not "good" or "bad"—it's just that they're not yours, and it's your energy the crystal will be working on or with to achieve its healing effects.

Incense is an easy way to cleanse crystals and purify your space. Burn frankincense or sandalwood sticks or cones.

METHODS OF CLEANSING

Outlined in the following pages are some of the traditional ways of cleansing your crystals. As with any method, intention is the key—before you begin, you need to be focused on the process of cleansing. So as you cleanse your crystal, think about what you are doing and how this action is releasing unwanted energies.

BRUSHING: A soft brush such as a makeup brush or a paint brush is good for removing dust that can build up on surfaces and delicate crevices of the stone.

PHYSICAL CLEANING: A little mild detergent mixed with water in a bowl, followed by a thorough rinse in clear water, will make crystals sparkle. (Don't use water if they are water-soluble crystals!)

RUNNING WATER: Hold your crystal under running water for a few minutes. It may need longer if it's been working hard or hasn't been cleansed for a long time. If you feel that it needs a lot of time, place the crystal in a bowl of water

Good Versus Bad Energy

There is no difference between good and bad energy—it is just energy, free of value judgments. For example, ruby or alexandrite can be used in a laser to target and kill an enemy, or a piece can be held to the sacral chakra to ease menstrual discomfort. Nuclear energy can run a hospital or destroy a city. We use judgmental contrasts like good and bad to try to make sense of our lives and define our world, but because everything is in a state of flux, our interpretations change from one moment to the next, according to context and viewpoint. Good and bad exist only in the moment in which we compare one thing with another. The next moment, good may become bad, or bad good.

in your sink and let the water run into the bowl for as long as necessary.

MOONLIGHT: Leave the crystal in moonlight, especially in a full moon, or leave it out during a new moon.

BURNING INCENSE OR A SMUDGE STICK: The smoke from frankincense, sandalwood, and sage is cleansing. You can burn either incense or a smudge stick (a small bunch of dried herbs burned during Native American cleansing rituals—see pages 176 and 193).

EARTH: Bury the crystal in the earth—when you unearth it a week or more later, it will be born anew. Different traditions around the world apply this technique in varying ways. One method is to bury it during a full moon and unearth it on a new moon.

CRYSTALLINE ENERGIES: Place the crystal on an amethyst bed, on a quartz cluster, or inside a geode and allow the crystalline energies to cleanse and clear it. A large amethyst bed can be like a vacation for your crystals. The question of how long you should leave them is a little open-ended. Crystals are like people—how long do you usually need to refresh and revitalize yourself? To know when a crystal is ready to

Fresh running water has an instant cleansing effect.

Placing a crystal in moonlight overnight aids cleansing.

Sunlight has a cleansing effect upon crystals.

work again, use your intuition—also, look for brightness and color returning to the crystal, which should no longer feel "clammy." Once you are used to working with crystals, you will find it easy to know when they are ready to go back to work.

SOUNDS: Chanting, drumming, or playing Tibetan bells or cymbals can clear unhelpful vibrations.

SUNLIGHT: You can cleanse your crystal by leaving it in sunlight and also dry your crystals in the sun after washing them. (Caution: Quartz crystals, especially crystal balls, will focus the sun's rays and so can be a fire risk. Take appropriate precautions.)

BREATH, LIGHT, OR REIKI: Breathing over your crystal helps to cleanse it—focus your mind, heart, and being through your breath, connecting your inner being to the outside. Reiki can also be practiced on crystals, and a meditation technique involving a visualization of light can be used, too: Still your mind and picture a bright light flowing from your brow chakra to the crystal in your hand, washing over it then filling the crystal. When it completely glows with light, slowly bring your focus away from the crystal and back to your surroundings.

A natural citrine crystal.

HOW TO WORK WITH CRYSTALS

Once you have selected and cleansed your crystals, you are ready to start working with them. Specific healing techniques are covered in detail in Chapter 5 (see page 175), but the following pages offer some easy methods that can be applied in many situations.

CARRYING AND HOLDING CRYSTALS

The easiest way of starting to work with crystals is to carry your selection with you. Crystals work all the time they are around you, so keeping them near you continually gives them the greatest opportunity to have an effect. You can carry any number you choose in any combination—there is no such thing as a bad mixture of crystals. Each one works by balancing something specific, whether of body, mind, or spirit. If this area is already in balance within you, then the crystals will do nothing other than look pretty. Play with them as you see fit and hold them whenever you feel the need. Sometimes just holding a crystal will provide instant relief in stressful situations. If you're carrying several crystals around with you and are drawn to just one or two, you can focus on the ones you notice.

Simply holding a crystal is the beginning of your healing relationship with it.

WEARING CRYSTALS

Remnants of crystal jewelry have been found at prehistoric sites around the world, and even today the employment of crystals and gems in jewelry is universal. This ancient method of working with crystals has the added benefit of their beauty adorning you while you gain the healing and spiritual properties of the crystals. As with carrying crystals, you can wear crystals in any combination you choose.

Where you wear crystals on your body is important. Not only do individual crystals affect particular areas of the body, but placing a crystal directly over a chakra can enhance its effect, as its energies are then carried through the body's energy system.

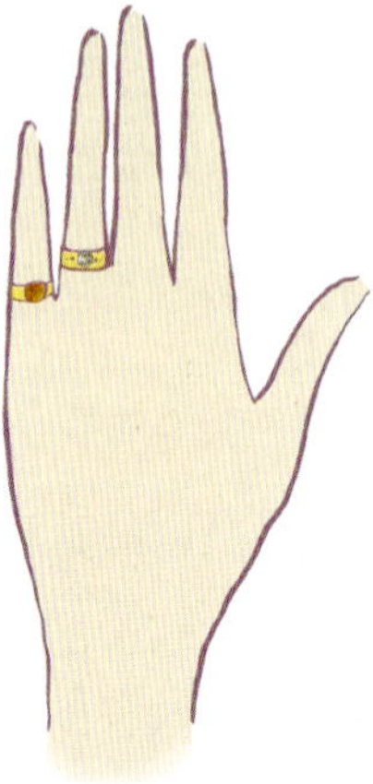

A citrine ring worn on the little finger can help the small intestine.

RINGS: A citrine ring worn on the little finger can help the small intestine, whereas a hematite ring could help relieve backache. The diamond engagement ring is worn on the third finger of the left hand, as this finger has always been believed to connect directly to the heart. (Interestingly, this finger is linked in ancient cultures to magic, mystery, and healing, and was known as the magic or medicine finger. It links to healing in Buddhism with the image of the Medicine Buddha, healing through his ring finger.)

NECKLACES: Wearing lapis lazuli, sapphire, or kyanite on a choker will speed the crystal's effect on the throat chakra. Emerald, jade, or rose quartz worn over the heart, or citrine or amber on a long chain or cord over the solar plexus, will also effect change in these areas.

EARRINGS AND TIARAS: When worn, for example, as earrings or tiaras, amethyst will help headaches, diamonds will boost psychic abilities, and rubies will aid wisdom and the understanding of problems.

When worn as earrings or in the hair, ruby promotes wisdom, diamond boosts the sixth sense, and amethyst helps headaches.

BUCKLES: Some cultures, such as the Native American peoples, have adorned belt buckles with jewels and crystals. This connects directly to the sacral chakra, which stores energy for when the body's energy system needs it in the future. Turquoise is traditional for buckles, which ties in with its quality as an all-round physical healer, its energy being available via the sacral chakra throughout the body.

LAYING ON OF STONES

Originating with shamanic practices, this time-honored healing application of crystals has been handed down through oral traditions the world over. The idea is simple—by placing crystals on specific areas of the body, their healing benefits are received directly at the required sites. For example, headaches would be treated by placing amethyst at the site of discomfort on the head. For digestive problems, a suitable crystal such as citrine would be placed on the stomach. Although there are variations of this approach, the principles are universal. Crystals are combined so that you end up with several crystals placed on different parts of the body or in the same area.

This methodology also links in with the body's energy system, so that treated areas may reflect the flow of energy to or from the site of physical discomfort rather than at the location itself. The healer might place crystals on the chakras, between them on meridians, and around the body in the aura to achieve a holistic healing of body, mind, and spirit, rather than working on the apparent physical symptoms. Because shamanic beliefs suggest that everything has a spirit, including illness, the holistic approach treats the spirit of the disease and not the symptoms. These treatments often end up with lots of crystals placed on the body, each having its own effect and also linking with other stones to create a much greater effect at all levels.

When receiving this type of treatment, you may notice one or more of the individual crystals or you may have an overall feeling. Each crystal may feel hot or cold, and either very heavy or so light that it seems not even there. You may have tingles, like electrical sensations, where the crystal is placed or in other areas of your body. You will often feel very calm and relaxed, and you may experience a feeling of heaviness as though you were rooted to the floor or bed.

Laying crystals on the seven chakra points is an ancient healing practice.

CRYSTAL ELIXIRS

A crystal elixir is water in which a crystal has been immersed. Simply drinking a glass of this enhanced water can improve your well-being. Traditionally, elixirs are seen as magical panaceas, bringing eternal youth and immortality. Although some of these claims are far-fetched, elixirs are effective healers. Simply prepared and as portable as a bottle of water, they are a powerful addition to the crystal healer's toolbox. For example:

- Moldavite elixir is a general tonic for the body and is helpful in the treatment of most minor illnesses.
- Amber elixir is one of the gentlest, most effective remedies for constipation.
- A turquoise elixir will help stress-related skin disorders.

Elixirs that you drink work from the inside out. Some are effective in the treatment of particular conditions (see Chapter 4). However, be aware of the warning "**Caution: NO ELIXIR**" that appears with some crystals—do **not** drink an elixir made from that crystal.

Amber elixir can benefit the digestive system.

Topical Elixirs

Some elixirs are applied topically—directly on the affected external area of the body, for example:

- Applied to the skin, an amber elixir can act as an antiseptic for cuts and grazes.
- After a day of too much sun you can bathe in a hematite elixir, or apply it locally to treat sunburn.

Preparing an Elixir

When making an elixir, it's important to think about what you are doing, focusing on the purpose of the elixir. Cleanse and wash your crystal, and then place it in water (preferably distilled or mineral water from a pure source, but water from your household tap will do). Cover the container and leave it in the refrigerator overnight. The elixir can be drunk (unless there is a caution not to drink it—see page 35) or applied topically over the next 24 hours. Some people like to enhance elixirs by leaving them in sunlight or moonlight or by surrounding them with quartz crystals to energize them.

PRACTICAL EXERCISE:
Spot the Difference

- Take three different crystals—say citrine, amethyst, and rose quartz—and place each in its own glass of water. Also have a glass of plain water as a control. Leave them to stand for 20–30 minutes.
- Now taste each one. Can you notice a difference? Usually citrine tastes slightly effervescent, amethyst tastes noticeably metallic, and rose quartz is slightly bland, a little like cheap bottled water. However, because everyone describes energy, sensations, and emotions with their own unique vocabulary, you may express these differently.

CRYSTAL DISPLAYS

Crystals work whenever they are around you, and even when you're not in the same space. They clear the air of negative energy after disputes or arguments, and energize the room, leaving it calm and relaxing—an ideal environment in which to unwind and rest, meditate, or focus your mind on work or problem-solving.

You can select different crystals for particular rooms in your house to create individual moods, and this approach could be linked to your interior design through choosing crystals by color or effect. To benefit, all you need to do is display crystals wherever they can be seen at home, or in your workplace on your desk, windowsill, shelves, or filing cabinets. Crystals can aid and promote so many aspects of your life that, once you start, you will find you add to your crystal collection regularly.

Placing crystals in your environment offers healing to all who share your space. Family, friends, pets, and plants will all benefit from the almost instant changes that crystals can produce in your surroundings.

OTHER BENEFITS

Crystals are also valuable in ways other than healing. Imagine the beautiful dinner table displays you could create with crystals. An ever-increasing number of brides are choosing crystals as wedding favors, to remind guests of their

Crystal displays create an everlasting ambience and make beautiful gifts.

special day. Many commercial companies are seeing crystals as a way to connect with their clients and customers. When the sugar-coated almonds are eaten or the promotional pen runs out of ink, the memory is lost, whereas a crystal is likely to last forever.

CONNECTING WITH YOUR CRYSTALS

The more you work with the same crystal to do the same thing, the better you and the crystal will **both** do it. It's like learning anything—the more you practice, the better you get. Some crystals want to do a bit of everything, while you are drawn to others for a specific task or need. It's a little like either being a jack-of-all-trades or being a brain surgeon. Both can be very helpful at different times but you wouldn't want Jack to operate on your head, nor would you want the surgeon to change the washer in your water tap!

Whatever your purpose in programming it, you and your crystal will be working as a team, so you need to relate to one another and communicate. Programming is about enhancing this communication. It relies on focusing the

Holding a crystal means you share your energy with it and begin to form a connection.

mind and your energy system to develop communication with the crystal's energy, in order to increase the crystal's effects in a specific area of healing or lifestyle change. If you select a crystal for a single purpose, then programming that crystal can speed its effects when you work with it.

Your Quartz Master Crystal

This will become a very special crystal for you. It will be a friend for life, sharing your personal healing and the work you do to help others. It will ease your path through all sorts of physical, mental, emotional, and spiritual situations in life. Therefore, when you select this crystal, take your time. Of course, you may find that when you go to a shop with the specific intent of selecting your quartz master crystal, a crystal may almost jump straight out at you. As always, trust your intuition and go for what you are drawn to. Or a particular crystal that you've had for years may be perfect for this task. Either way, it shouldn't be so small that it feels fussy to work with, or so big that it is too heavy or awkward. Ideally, it should be a good "hand-size" clear quartz crystal.

A quartz master crystal

PRACTICAL EXERCISE:
Programming Your Quartz Master Crystal

Once you have selected a special crystal to be your quartz master crystal and you have cleansed it, you need to connect to it.

- First, take a good look at it. Observe the shapes, colors, and play of light. Now hold it in your hands, close your eyes, and notice how it feels. Become aware of the smooth, flat, sharp, and pointed areas. Be aware of any feelings you have, such as physical sensations in your hands or subtle feelings within you. Hold your crystal very close to your ear and listen to it—crystals have a physical vibration, which most people can hear, like the sound of a sea shell to your ear. Taste it by placing it against the taste buds on the tip of your tongue. Finally, smell the crystal: Many people can sense the unique aromas of particular crystals.
- While holding the crystal, focus your mind on this being your quartz master crystal. Think about what it will be doing, helping you first on your personal healing journey, then healing others. Sit quietly and imagine (or pretend—it works just as well) that this thought in your mind is going deep into your crystal. Do this for 10 to 20 minutes.
- Ideally, repeat this daily for two weeks. You will find that it will take you less time each day to connect to the same crystal. Each day, ask your crystal to be your quartz master crystal, with all that this entails. Carry it with you as much as possible. If you need to leave it alone, place it where it won't be disturbed. Ideally, you should be the only person to have contact with your quartz master crystal during this time. You can apply it to any of the healing techniques in Chapter 5 for healing yourself. After two weeks you can start working with this crystal to help other people, too.

CRYSTAL MEDITATION

Crystals can promote the various stages of meditation by helping to focus and clear the mind. There are many crystals that support meditation, such as kyanite to help you get started and fluorite to still your mind. And the still state of mind that is induced by meditation promotes the spiritual and physical effects of crystal healing.

When you meditate with crystals, your experience will differ from day to day, and depend on the crystals you work with. This is normal. One day you'll feel relaxed, another energized. You may be happy and peaceful or sad, edgy, and agitated. Accept these feelings and don't block unpleasant ones—they will pass.

After a short time of meditating each day with your crystals, all sorts of interesting things will start to happen. You will notice that you are feeling better, healthier, and stronger emotionally. You'll feel more at peace, relaxed, and energized. Your mind will be calmer, and you will do everything a little better and more efficiently. Slowly your life will improve.

Meditation has probably received more scientific study than any other alternative practice, because it is practiced by scientists and doctors as well as alternatively minded people the world over. It has been shown to have a great number of psychological and physiological benefits.

White and green fluorite

Physical Benefits of Meditation

Regular meditation produces genuine physiological effects, such as deep relaxation, and a wakefulness or highly alert mental state. It counteracts the effects of stress, such as headaches and digestive disorders.

Not only does meditation reduce stress, but it also increases your ability to cope with stress. It enhances the natural relaxation response, helping the "fight-or-flight" response to subside (our modern lifestyle often prevents this, resulting in 21st-century stress and its related symptoms). This is reflected in many physiological changes, including a fall in the body's metabolic rate (shown in the fall in oxygen consumption and heart rate), lowered blood pressure in those with high blood pressure, and reduced blood levels of stress chemicals (which include lactate, cortisol, and adrenaline).

You can meditate in a crystal circle, which can also help create a sacred space around you.

Meditation has numerous benefits for general health and has been shown to help insomnia, hypertension, headaches and migraines, chronic pain, allergies, asthma, and stress-related skin, digestive, and nervous system disorders. It stimulates the immune system, speeding up recovery from illness, infection, or surgery.

It makes nerve impulses travel quicker, helps body fluids to move more freely, and opens air passages, making breathing easier. It boosts the digestive system and improves the circulation of blood, resulting in a more efficient distribution of nutrients and elimination of waste products.

Meditation has also been found to increase blood levels of certain substances (such as GABA, melatonin, DHEA) that help to maintain health and prevent disease. In fact, serious meditation practice—at least an hour a day—will, after several weeks or so, lead to a general improvement in health and well-being for most people.

Psychological Benefits of Meditation

The state induced by meditation promotes psychological health, reducing anxiety and susceptibility to stress, and increasing confidence, happiness, empathy, alertness, openness to experience, perceptual sensitivity, creativity, and the ability to concentrate and perform cognitive tasks.

In effect, meditation helps to balance the left and right hemispheres of the brain. This is not just logic and intuition, but also each side of the brain controls the motor coordination and muscular responses of the opposite side of the body. If this is out of balance, then so is your body, leading to physical tension, which can create headaches, stress, and numerous physical symptoms such as digestive disorders; it is said that anxious people "tie themselves in knots." Meditation balances left and right—thoughts and feelings, logic and intuition.

PRACTICAL EXERCISE:
Meditating with Crystals

- Find a quiet space and allow yourself to breathe, center, and calm yourself. This quiet space can be simply inside you, but to start with it is easier to create a place in both time and space. Make a time when you won't be disturbed. Switch off the telephone or put up a "do not disturb" sign.
- Put on some gentle, relaxing music, light a candle if you wish, and place crystals around you.
- Choose one crystal to focus on, and allow yourself to explore it with all your senses. Connect with the crystal and be aware of any sensations and feelings, whether physical, emotional, mental, or spiritual.
- Stay with this process for at least ten minutes, but keep going for up to an hour if you have the time. The important thing is to repeat the meditation daily.

Kyanite

A Holistic Practice

The interdependence of physical, mental, emotional, and spiritual health is reflected in the benefits of meditation. For example, the stillness of mind that meditation produces in times of stress is known to enhance the performances of dancers, tennis players, actors, football players, and motorcycle racers—think what it could do for you.

Meditating with crystals helps to still the mind.

CRYSTALS FOR MEDITATION

By making us less judgmental and more open to experience, meditation creates the right state of mind for crystal healing. All of the many types of meditation promote both the spiritual and healing effects of any crystal. All crystals support meditation by acting as a point of focus, and many also enhance specific aspects of the meditative process.

Tree agate

AGATE aids self diagnosis and visualization.

AMETHYST helps you to center and expand the meditation experience; hold one in each hand.

AMETRINE speeds the meditation process, so you get to your own deepest state in less time.

Apophyllite

APOPHYLLITE promotes reflection.

BLUE QUARTZ helps you reach a state of bliss, enlightenment, or peak experience.

CARNELIAN provides inner strength in long meditations and is especially suitable for retreats.

Blue quartz

CELESTITE helps you to identify and promote your dreams, ambitions, and goals in life.

Celestite

Charoite

Fire opal

Hessonite

Kunzite

Malachite

CHAROITE brings clarity to the mind and stillness to the body.

FIRE OPAL aids visions.

FLUORITE clears and stills the mind, bringing focus.

GARNET connects to the heart and base chakras, grounding emotion and the meditative experience.

GOLDEN CALCITE aids healing visualizations.

HESSONITE helps you go to the "next level" from wherever you are.

IMPERIAL TOPAZ advances enlightenment, the universal connection to everything, giving a feeling of oneness or bliss, and enhances visualization and distant healing.

KUNZITE is centering, helps you reach a deep state of meditation, and promotes intuition and creativity.

KYANITE helps you get started with the process of meditation.

MALACHITE is good for looking deep within yourself, aiding the release of emotions, and bringing stillness.

Morganite

MORGANITE helps to fill the space in your heart created by loss or grief and helps expand your meditation to send out love from your heart to the world.

PERIDOT promotes the search for enlightenment.

Petrified wood

PETALITE helps you stay grounded during and after meditation and bring the experience into your everyday life.

PETRIFIED WOOD connects to past lives.

Pietersite

PIETERSITE encourages visions and supports visualization during guided meditation.

PREHNITE helps you to get started with the process of meditation.

Quartz crystal

QUARTZ CRYSTAL supports all meditations and each stage of the process.

RED JASPER keeps you grounded while promoting the meditative state.

RUBY creates a connection between the base, heart, and crown chakras, promoting peak experiences, bliss, or the feeling of connection to everything around you.

Red jasper

Smoky quartz

Spirit quartz

Tanzanite

Vanadanite

SMOKY QUARTZ clears the mind and gives auric protection during deep meditations.

SPIRIT QUARTZ aids insights into family and community problems.

TANZANITE facilitates visualization and understanding gained during meditations.

TIGER'S EYE supports distant healing.

TITANIUM QUARTZ helps you see many possibilities.

TURQUOISE grounds peak experiences.

VERDELITE (a green variety of tourmaline) aids visualization.

VANADINITE creates a state of "no mind" (when thoughts are absent), aids visualization, and helps circular breathing (inhaling while exhaling).

WHITE CALCITE makes it easier to find answers.

CHAPTER 3

THE BODY'S ENERGY SYSTEM

This chapter explores the chakras, the body's essential centers of power, and the aura, our unique energy field. Discover here how crystals heal chakras, and the seven key crystals that work with each of the seven chakras—essential for your crystal tool kit.

CHAKRAS: ENERGY HOT SPOTS

Imagine energy flowing through pathways within the body, a little like blood flows through arteries and veins. Where these energy pathways cross each other, there is a concentration of power—an energy hot spot. And where many of the energy pathways cross each other, there is a major energy hot spot. The energy pathways are known as meridians (or, in Indian tradition, nadis) and the energy hot spots as chakras.

The other major component of the body's energy system is the aura, an etheric energy field surrounding the body. Energy emanates from the chakras into the aura and back through the chakras to your body, giving you a psychic sense of your surroundings. You can affect the flow of this energy by concentrating your mind and working with crystals, colors, and fragrances.

ENERGY EBB AND FLOW

The chakras are the areas of the highest density of energy and therefore the easiest places to exchange energy with the outside world. These are the places through which we control the flow of our energy, both internally and externally. To those people who can see energy, the chakras look like spinning balls or wheels of light—hence the name, which comes from a Sanskrit word meaning wheel or circle.

Most Eastern traditions describe a chakra system consisting of seven major chakras, with each one associated with an area of the body (see opposite).

Locating the Chakras

7 Crown:
Top of the head

6 Brow:
Center of the forehead, above the eyebrows (also known as the third eye)

5 Throat:
Center of the throat

4 Heart:
Center of the chest

3 Solar plexus:
Behind the soft cartilage at the bottom of the breastbone

2 Sacral:
Just below the navel

1 Base:
Coccyx (at the base of the spine)

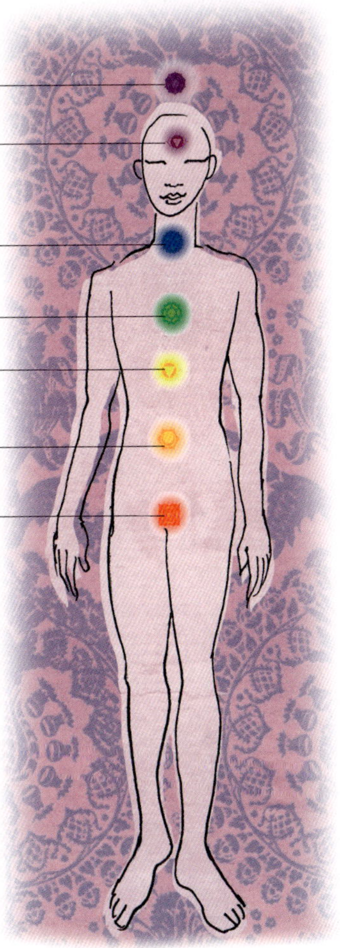

See page 57 for a basic set of crystals that can balance the chakras.

The chakras are numbered from the first chakra, which is the base chakra, up to the seventh chakra at the crown. The chakras create a pathway of spinning energy hot spots along the axis of the body.

Chakras go in and out of balance and alignment naturally, fluctuating with everyday highs and lows. The little stresses of life, minor illnesses, emotions, and even your thoughts can change the equilibrium of your chakra system. Your energy, and therefore your chakras, are influenced by everything you do. When you are feeling anxious or unwell, or are not following your path in life, your chakras may shift way out of alignment and, if left untreated, take a long time to realign.

HOW CRYSTALS HEAL CHAKRAS

A healthy, balanced chakra has energy flowing through it. Where there is dis-ease (when the body is not in a state of "ease" or wellness), the energy slows or becomes blocked. Working with your crystals directly on your chakras can heal and prevent dis-ease, thus aiding physical, mental, emotional, and spiritual health. A balanced chakra system allows you to sense the world around you, avoid the unwanted effects of stress, and remain emotionally calm so you can live your life to the full.

Working with crystals is one of the simplest and best ways of balancing and healing your chakras. By placing a crystal on a chakra, the crystal focuses healing energy directly on the area concerned, which naturally calms and heals the body, emotions, mind, and spirit as needed. For example, malachite placed on the heart chakra helps to soothe emotions, citrine on the solar plexus chakra can ease digestive disorders, and carnelian positioned on the sacral chakra can give a boost of energy to help you deal with changes and cope with stressful events. Each crystal constantly emits a unique healing energy. Some of these energies marry happily to a specific chakra. Every crystal will help one, some, or even all of the body's energy hot spots.

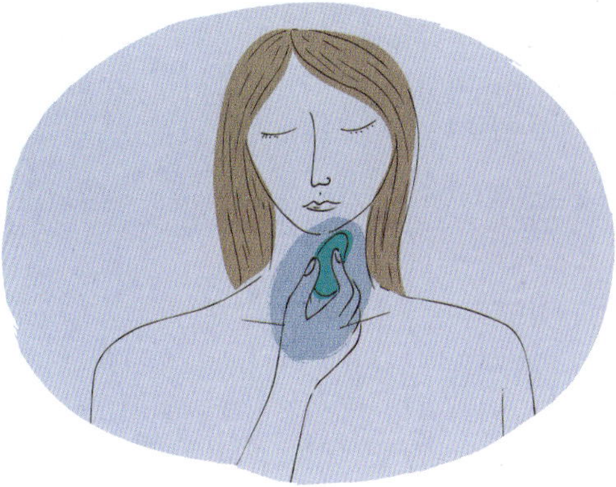

Holding turquoise to the throat area can aid communication.

All crystals work through a balancing process. Imagine a tube with water running through it. This tube can appear blocked and therefore imbalanced for several reasons: if only a small amount of fluid is entering it, if there is a blockage, if the walls become swollen making the internal diameter smaller, or if too much water is flooding into the tube's entrance. In each example, only a trickle of liquid may emerge. In a similar way, different crystals suited to each chakra will unblock energy stuck in the chakra from one of these causes.

Another way of looking at it is that by placing a crystal with similar energy to the healthy energy state of a chakra on or near the hot spot, the crystal "reminds" the chakra how it is to be healthy and the chakra naturally falls back into balance. A similar technique is used in meditative healing in which we visualize what it felt like when we were healthy and the body physically replicates the image.

Chakra Associated Concepts

BASE
Survival, health, abundance, connection to earth, moving forward in life

SACRAL
Connection to other people, creativity, energy, confidence

SOLAR PLEXUS
Physical center, personal power, emotions

HEART
Love, safety, trust, adventure, relationships

THROAT
Communication, expression, responsibility, freedom, leadership

BROW
Mind, ideas, thoughts, dreams, psychic abilities

CROWN
Spirituality, connection to universe, imagination, awareness, optimism

FOLLOW THE RAINBOW

With nearly 35 years' experience as a crystal teacher and healer, I have chosen the crystals for the chakra set in this book for simplicity and effect. It's much easier to recall which crystal goes where with a simple color coding that ties in with the chakras. Therefore, the mantra here is to follow the rainbow: red, orange, yellow, green, blue, indigo, and violet, from the base chakra upward. Each crystal is selected because it ties in with this color code and is effective and available from any good crystal shop or online store. Although there are many other crystal combinations and substitutions, these work for the majority of people most of the time.

- RED JASPER for the base is solid.
- CARNELIAN for the sacral is dynamic.
- CITRINE for the solar plexus is a wonderful multipurpose gem.
- MALACHITE for the heart doesn't mess about. Many healers will recommend aventurine or rose quartz as a general crystal for the heart center—those are soft and gentle, but malachite smashes through emotional blocks like a sledgehammer, speeding up recovery.
- BLUE LACE AGATE for the throat is calming yet direct.
- LAPIS LAZULI for the brow is a formidable opener of awareness.
- AMETHYST provides the spiritual connection from the crown.

All these crystals also have multiple healing applications and are an excellent addition to your crystal chakra healing tool box. I will discuss each chakra in detail in Chapter 4 (see page 65), but first, let's look at the rest of the body's energy system.

Crystals for Chakra Healing

Base: *Red jasper*

Sacral: *Carnelian*

Solar plexus: *Citrine*

Heart: *Malachite*

Throat: *Blue lace agate*

Brow: *Lapis lazuli*

Crown: *Amethyst*

THE AURA: THE BODY'S ENERGY FIELD

Your aura—the etheric energy field surrounding you—should not be thought of as something separate, because your energy system is a complete entity. It is as much a part of you as your hands, head, and hormones. Energy flows from your body through your chakras into your aura and beyond to the outside world. At the same time it also flows in the reverse direction, from the outside world into you.

The aura is the first line of defense of the body's energy system in much the same way as the skin is the first line of defense of the immune system. When your aura is strong and healthy, you are less likely to become ill and are more likely to attract friends, develop relationships, and experience a happy life.

The aura plays several important roles in crystal chakra healing, as it connects you to your environment and all the external factors such as people and events, as well as pollutants that affect the body, mind, spirit, and emotions. As you will see in Chapter 5, the aura is always included in full treatments.

The aura extends around the head and whole body.

THE LAYERS OF THE AURA

The aura is roughly elliptical in shape and is made up of seven layers: the physical aura (closest to the body), etheric aura, emotional aura, vital aura, astral aura, lower mental plane, and higher mental plane (above the head).

THE PHYSICAL AURA: Working outward from your skin, the first layer, or physical aura, is very narrow, extending no more than ⅜ in/1 cm from the skin. It is very difficult to separate the sense of this layer of the aura from the sensation you feel when a slight breeze ruffles the hairs on your arm. The physical aura is your connection to all the energies surrounding you—your energy communication channel.

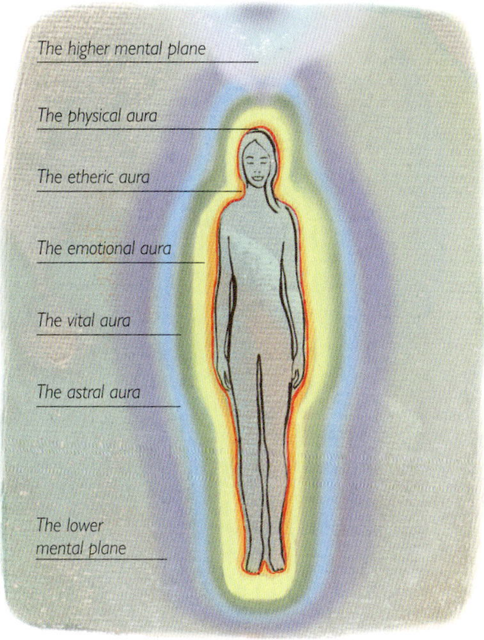

THE ETHERIC AURA: The second layer, the etheric aura, is one of the easiest to sense with your pendulum or hand. It starts about ⅜ in/1 cm out from the body and is about ¾–1½ in/2–4 cm thick. It is the first part of the aura people see when beginning to see auras, always appearing with a slight gray or

PRACTICAL EXERCISE:
Sensing Your Etheric Aura

- Hold the flat palm of your hand or your pendulum about 3–4 in/8–10 cm from a friend's arm. (You can use your other arm instead, but it's much easier to do this with someone else.)
- Focus your mind on finding and sensing the etheric aura and slowly move your hand or pendulum toward the arm.
- If you are using your hand, you should feel a change in sensation, such as warmth or coolness, a slight physical resistance, pins and needles, or an itchy palm. If working with a pendulum, it should start to move. The direction of movement is not important at this stage—it is any change that you are looking for. Whatever sensation you have or movement you notice will be subtle and you will need to be very focused to appreciate it, but it is something that everyone can easily find.

purple tint. It is a protective barrier to the physical body, defending against dis-ease that may be held in the outer areas of the aura.

THE EMOTIONAL AURA: Extending a further 1½–2¼ in/4–6 cm, this is the layer in your energy field where you hold emotion. Here, like attracts like, and so, over time, good feelings tend to group together, as do bad ones. Imagine the bad emotions as dark bits of energy. As they group together they exert a "pull" a bit like gravity on other dark energy. They slowly grow into larger masses. These draw energy from wherever they can, including other layers of the aura, the surroundings, and the body, creating a feeling around the person. We've all experienced this occasionally in somebody else. The sense that someone is draining you or you don't feel comfortable around them is stemming from these dark blobs of energy in their emotional aura. When the good emotions group themselves together in much the same way, the feeling around a person becomes light and welcoming. This helps to attract friends and relationships of a healthy nature. We all know people who it feels good to be around.

THE VITAL AURA: As its name suggests, the vital aura is essential to health. All dis-ease is said to appear in this part of the aura well before there are any physical symptoms in the body. Everything that has happened to you in your life is recorded here, and this is the region psychics who specialize in "aura readings" look at to see into your past, present, and future. Unlike most of the other layers, which alter little, the vital aura changes size and color continuously, according to your health, moods, feelings, and emotions. With a little practice you can even expand and contract it at will.

THE ASTRAL AURA: Another layer that changes size, and also shape, dramatically, the astral aura is involved in out-of-body experiences including astral travel and projection. It acts as a bridge between you and the rest of the universe—it is where you start to sense your surroundings.

THE LOWER MENTAL PLANE: This layer can be imagined as an elliptical membrane surrounding each person. Less than 1⁄32 in/1 mm thick, it is the edge of the aura and the boundary of your energy system. Occasionally, holes develop in the lower mental plane, which can lead to an oozing of energy, making you lethargic and prone to minor illness. These holes can be healed by "combing" a quartz crystal through the aura (see pages 189 and 191).

THE HIGHER MENTAL PLANE: There is much debate about this final layer of the aura. It appears to hover over the head, about 1½ in/4 cm above the lower mental plane. Many people think that it is connected to the lower mental plane, but I see it as your connection to spirit, God, or universal energy. The higher mental plane is the layer that is most susceptible to influence from things other people say, such as when, as a child, you may have been told to stop speaking to your "imaginary friend." The more you use your ability to contact the spirit world, the easier it becomes. When this has become normal for you, you will see the guiding hand of the universe all around you.

PRACTICAL EXERCISE:
Changing Your Vital Aura

- The next time you go to the grocery store, try contracting your aura. Think about it shrinking smaller and smaller, coming in close all around you. Picture yourself shrinking in size. Imagine you are invisible. Notice what happens as you do your shopping. You'll find people just don't notice you, bump into your cart, and generally seem to ignore you.
- Before you go to the store again, try expanding your aura. Picture it growing and filling the whole room. Imagine you are growing bigger. This time you will find that people notice you. They won't bump into you and you'll even have some extra personal space in the line at the checkout. This expansion of the vital aura is what makes stars (pop stars, that is, not the ones in space!), who can seem to "fill" an auditorium with their presence. In fact, it is their aura that is filling the auditorium.

CRYSTALS FOR THE AURA

All the crystals you ever work with are already in your aura. You can work with them in several ways (explained in more detail in Chapter 5, pages 186–187):

- By brushing down or combing the aura to remove unwanted dark blobs of energy
- By placing crystals around you—for example, you could sit in a circle or oval of crystals—with differing effects depending on the type of crystal employed
- By holding crystals and visualizing the effects on your aura
- By rotating a crystal or pendulum in your hand, clockwise to cleanse the aura and counterclockwise to reenergize it

Aqua aura

Amazonite

These are the best crystals to use:

Agate	Jasper
Amazonite	Labradorite
Amethyst	Petalite
Ametrine	Rutile
Aqua aura	Titanium quartz
Citrine	Tourmaline
Diamond	Zircon
Garnet	

Rutile

CHAPTER 4

THE CHAKRAS

In the following pages are detailed profiles of the seven chakras, showing how they affect us emotionally, mentally, physically, and spiritually, and which crystals to work with to best experience their powerful healing benefits.

HEALING THE BASE CHAKRA

The base chakra, also known as the first chakra, is located at the base of the spine. It is the survival center, supporting strength, determination, and the things that nurture us such as our friends and family. In certain traditions, such as ayurveda and hatha yoga, it is regarded as the place where the resting kundalini is stored. It is the center through which we experience our connection to the earth and the earth plane while we are living this life. A healthy base chakra will keep you grounded and help you move forward in life.

LOCATION: Base of the spine (coccyx)

CRYSTAL: Red jasper

COLOR: Red

FRAGRANCE ASSOCIATION: Patchouli

KEYWORDS: Survival, health, abundance, connection to the earth, change, strength, family, security, nurture, assertiveness, determination, passion, practical matters, tradition, endings and new beginnings

EMOTIONAL/MENTAL HEALING: An unbalanced base chakra can prevent you from advancing in life. When it's blocked, nothing seems to happen. The lack of balance prevents the release of grief and other restricting emotions that hold you back. Everyone needs time to grieve, but this should always be a process of release rather than something to hold on to. Death is about change—not just for the person who dies but also for the relatives and friends they leave behind. All change brings opportunity and a fresh start. Without releasing grief and holding onto feelings such as sorrow and guilt, any new projects you start may never quite work or come to fruition. This prevents abundance—not only material but abundance on a deep soul level, of sensitive feelings and happy emotions. You feel unfulfilled. Slowly this has an emotional effect. You start to feel as if nothing is working or worthwhile and no one is on your side. You become stressed, a myriad of apparently unrelated physical symptoms begin to appear, and low-level depression sets in. You can feel as if you have lost a connection but to what you often are not sure. The dysfunction of your base chakra prevents you from appreciating the nurturing things in life. You can feel distanced from family and friends and unsettled. As you start to feel alone, insecurity can set in, leading to anxiety and panic attacks. In extreme circumstances, addictions, phobias, and obsessions can develop.

PHYSICAL HEALING: When the base chakra is out of balance, common symptoms appear, such as chronic lower-back pain, varicose veins, sciatica, water retention, rectal and anal problems, constipation, diarrhea, some fertility issues such as impotence, and immune disorders. The base chakra also affects the health of the groin, hips, pelvis, lower end of the digestive system, legs, knees, ankles, and feet.

A healthy base chakra will strengthen your connection to the home, family, and friends.

SPIRITUAL HEALING: The base chakra connects you to the earth. In one sense this is rational, mental grounding, as in your link to the planet; keeping your feet on the ground rather than your head in the sky. In another way, it's bringing all your spiritual knowledge and experience into your everyday life, living in the present moment and experiencing every second of your existence. Part of this process can involve development workshops and classes, but many people go to these, have enlightening experiences, and then simply go back to their everyday lives, maybe tell their friends about the weekend, and… nothing. A healthy base chakra enables you to take the experiences and skills you have acquired and use them in your everyday life. This brings positive change in small manageable doses, leading to happiness.

LIFESTYLE: A balanced base chakra can help you move forward in life, change career, accept opportunities, and run with the ball when it falls in your hands. It promotes a healthy sense of security and confidence, allowing you to give and receive nurture, stand up for yourself when you need to, take advantage of all that life offers, and succeed in whatever you do.

ALTERNATIVE CRYSTALS: Hematite, black obsidian, smoky quartz, snowflake obsidian, red calcite, falcon's eye, zircon, mookaite, black banded agate, jet, black opal, petrified wood

HEALING BENEFITS

Balancing the base chakra stimulates the flow of energy through the body's whole energy system, which can have a beneficial effect on many chronic conditions throughout the body. It also helps to build up energy that is stored in the sacral chakra for when it is needed. By removing anxiety and stress, this healthy flow of energy allows positive changes to occur in your life. It facilitates the release of unwanted and unneeded emotions and thoughts that can block your path and prevent you from following your destiny.

How to Tell If Your Base Chakra Is Out of Balance

When the base chakra is out of balance, energy doesn't flow or moves very slowly, leading to a stagnation of life's movement: You can feel stuck in a rut and find it difficult to release emotions that become trapped. Sometimes a loss, such as a death or broken relationship, has occurred, and a failure to release the associated emotions leads to dysfunction in this energy hot spot. Common symptoms include:

- Chronic lower-back pain
- Sciatica
- Varicose veins
- Water retention
- Constipation or diarrhea
- Rectal and anal problems
- Fertility issues such as impotence
- Immune disorders
- Feelings of insecurity
- Phobias
- Depression, anxiety, or panic attacks

CRYSTALS FOR THE BASE CHAKRA

You can work with crystals to balance and heal the base chakra by placing the crystal directly on the energy center on your body (see page 53), carrying it with you all the time or, if suitable, taping it to your body with surgical tape. You can also try meditating with your chosen crystal and putting it by your bed or under your pillow at night. For more information on these and other healing techniques, refer to Chapter 5.

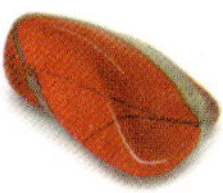

Red jasper

Falcon's eye

Hematite

Zircon

Black obsidian

Mookaite

Smoky quartz

Black banded agate

Snowflake obsidian

Jet

Black opal

Red calcite

Petrified wood

RED JASPER

Red opaque variety of quartz colored by iron oxide inclusions.

Common sources: Brazil, India

Astrological associations: Taurus, Aries

Chakra: Base

Healing qualities: Aids rebirth—that is, the idea of death and rebirth, or the end of something leading to a new beginning, bringing fresh opportunities and a fresh start. Promotes the survival instinct and boosts dream recall and astral travel. It is particularly helpful in meditations, helping to reduce stress, worry, and anxiety. Offers protection, especially in combination with jet.

Physical benefits: General tonic for the body, helping to prevent illness.

HEMATITE

Metallic silver-gray when polished, black and reddish brown masses, botryoidal forms, rosettes, layered "plates," rhombohedral and black tabular crystals.

Common sources: Brazil, Morocco, UK

Astrological associations: Aries, Aquarius

Chakra: Base

Healing qualities: One of the most grounding crystals, hematite helps things happen. It deflects negativity, bringing courage and strength in times of need, allowing mental processes to function and encouraging clear thinking. This allows you to make choices and move forward with confidence, reducing stress in the process. Failing to make choices is a common cause of both insomnia and poor memory recall, so hematite will help with both these conditions. It also helps the yin and yang energy balance—the male and female energies within each of us—enhancing personal magnetism and attracting love. In meditation hematite aids grounding, letting you bring the meditative experience into your everyday life. It can also be helpful for anyone involved with numbers, such as accountants and the self-employed.

Physical benefits: Good for blood and spine. Helps anemia, blood clots, cramp, disorders of the spleen, multiple sclerosis, backache, jet lag, fever (when drunk as an elixir), and sunburn (when applied as a topical elixir). Assists healing of bone fractures. Eases travel, sea, and air sickness. Improves mental dexterity with numbers.

BLACK OBSIDIAN

Pure black natural volcanic glass.

Common sources: Mexico, USA

Astrological association: Sagittarius

Chakra: Base

Healing qualities: Boosts intuition and creativity, promoting psychic abilities, in particular scrying. By improving awareness through intuition, it is also protective, grounding, and a focus for male energy. It connects with and enhances all types of shamanic healing.

Physical benefits: Good for stomach and digestion; helps digestive disorders.

SMOKY QUARTZ

Brown or black variety of quartz colored by natural radiation from the earth.

Common alternative name: Carnigorm

Common sources: Brazil, Madagascar, USA

Astrological associations: Capricorn, Sagittarius

Chakra: Base

Healing qualities: Perhaps the key crystal for releasing pent-up emotion such as grief, fear, anger, resentment, or frustration. It aids the flow of energy, both through your own energy system and to others through any energy-healing modality, such as Reiki or spiritual healing. This flow of energy through the body enhances many aspects, from mental activity to physical expression, often releasing depression and negativity, which leads to a relaxed state. In turn, this allows your life to advance. Smoky quartz is a protective crystal, sending back negative thoughts and feelings to their source, and so it can be viewed as speeding up the laws of karma. It is employed extensively to bring protection during ceremonies and to boost intuition and male energy, increasing survival instincts. A grounding crystal, it aids dream interpretation and meditation. It also discourages obsessive behavior such as overspending.

Physical benefits: Good for legs, knees, ankles, hands, feet, vitality, and sexual energy, and helps treat nervous speech impediments.

SNOWFLAKE OBSIDIAN

Black obsidian with inclusions of white phenocryst.

Common source: USA

Astrological association: Virgo

Chakra: Base

Healing qualities: Helps to release anger, resentment, and unhelpful behavior patterns and reduce loneliness, bringing peace of mind. It facilitates meditation and assists in purification of the body's energy system, detoxing the body, mind, and emotions.

Physical benefits: Unblocks the meridian linking the stomach and sinuses. Also helps with eyes (when drunk as an elixir), eyesight, veins, bones, and skin (when drunk as an elixir). Helps acalculia and dyscalculia.

RED CALCITE

Red variety of calcite found in masses; the building block of lime and marble.

Common source: Mexico

Astrological association: Cancer

Chakra: Base

Healing qualities: A grounding crystal that calms physical energy, reducing anxiety and panic attacks. Helps in the treatment of ADHD (attention deficit hyperactivity disorder) and OCD (obsessive-compulsive disorder)

Physical benefits: Good for kidneys, pancreas, and spleen.

FALCON'S EYE

Quartz has replaced asbestos while retaining the fibrous structure of the original asbestos crystal, giving the characteristic chatoyancy effect shown by all the tiger's eye family.

Common alternative name: Red tiger's eye

Common source: South Africa

Astrological association: Capricorn

Chakra: Base

Healing qualities: Brings heated emotions under control, thereby promoting practicality in all areas. When you become calm and start to deal with the things around you, you automatically grow in confidence, which boosts self-esteem and sexuality.

Physical benefits: Good for the reproductive system. Helps sunburn.

ZIRCON

Short, square prismatic crystals, often octahedral; colors include red, brown, green, gray, yellow, and colorless.

Common source: Pakistan

Astrological associations: Virgo, Leo, Sagittarius

Chakra: Base

Healing qualities: Zircon's calming energy brings out the best in you, boosting self-esteem, personal magnetism, wisdom, toughness, stamina, dependability, and easing depression. It helps to attract soul mates, leading to better, more intense, and lasting relationships. Zircon also enhances the quality of purity in your life and can be beneficial in the treatment of insomnia.

Physical benefits: Good for the pineal gland, aura, bones, and muscles. Helps allergies, sciatica, vertigo, and poisoning.

MOOKAITE

Patterned red and cream variety of jasper.

Common source: Australia

Astrological association: Leo

Chakra: Base

Healing qualities: Helps change how you see the world around you, allowing you to move forward while staying grounded. A protective and calming crystal, it boosts creativity and self-esteem, assisting the flow of new ideas and making it easier to make decisions. Mookaite promotes friendship and communication, dispelling loneliness, depression, and fear. It enhances both the dream and meditative states. It is particularly helpful for young mothers trying to balance life's stresses, seeking a new job, or coping with childbirth.

Physical benefits: Helps with thyroid imbalance, weight loss, stomach conditions, hernia, water retention.

BLACK BANDED AGATE

Variety of agate showing black and white banding.

Common source: India

Astrological association: Capricorn

Chakra: Base

Healing qualities: Brings balance to the female and male aspects of your energy system. With equilibrium between these yin and yang energies you can see things differently, remove bias, and find new answers to old problems, effecting change and promoting new beginnings. It also boosts endurance.

Physical benefits: Good for digestion; eases death and the dying process.

JET

The fossilized remains of trees.

Common sources: Canada, UK

Astrological association: Capricorn

Chakra: Base

Healing qualities: Promotes energy with calmness, enhancing the yin and yang energy balance and sexual energy, and giving protection from illness, violence, and, in combination with red jasper, psychic attack. This expels depression and fear, allowing you to move forward into abundance. Jet is valuable in the acquisition of wealth.

Physical benefits: Helps migraine, epilepsy, swollen glands, stomach ache, and the common cold.

BLACK OPAL

Forms black masses. Sometimes shows iridescence (fire) in various colors.

Common sources: Australia, Hungary, USA

Astrological associations: Scorpio, Sagittarius, Cancer

Chakra: Base

Healing qualities: Gets you moving but keeps you grounded at the same time. It helps fight depression and is beneficial in scrying and iridology.

Physical benefits: Good for digestion, eyesight, and fertility.

PETRIFIED WOOD

Fossilized trees, in which organic material has been replaced by one or more minerals. These are usually agate, chalcedony, and quartz, or sometimes opal, but many other minerals can be present. May be brown or any color of natural wood.

Common sources: Worldwide, especially Madagascar, USA

Astrological association: Leo

Chakra: Base

Healing qualities: A wonderful crystal for dealing with stress—it is grounding, soothes the emotions, and helps to bring mental balance, allowing you to relax and look at the bigger picture. It also helps you to access past life experiences.

Physical benefits: Helps arthritis, infection, allergies, hay fever, and conditions caused by pollutants. Good for bones and promotes longevity.

Crystal Clinic

When Jane arrived for her first healing session, she was suffering from lower-back pain, which she accepted was her "weak spot," and insomnia. She felt constantly tired and lethargic, which she put down to the pain and lack of sleep. After a brief discussion I learned that she was trying to change her career but things kept getting in the way, such as her partner losing his job and her mother becoming ill.

With her lying on her stomach, I placed red jasper on her base chakra with a quartz star (see pages 182–183) around it. I arranged all the other base chakra crystals in a circle around this. I worked with the master quartz crystal first for pain relief and then on the red jasper and quartz star. She reported that the pain in her lower back had gone and she felt heat around the whole base area but specifically below each crystal.

She was given red jasper and hematite to work with during the week, keeping them near her all the time—placing them on her bedside table or in her bed at night—and holding them whenever she felt the need. Where possible, she used a focused meditation while holding them, and when this was not practical she simply played with them in her hands and held them to any areas of discomfort. Each morning she cleansed them under running water.

The following week she returned, reporting that the pain had returned after five days but that she was sleeping significantly better and felt less tired. I repeated the treatment, but this time without the additional base chakra crystals, and I gave her black obsidian to work with during the week.

The third week she reported that she was pain-free, was sleeping well, and had a job interview (she later accepted the job). I applied a basic chakra crystal set (see page 57) to help maintain the newly found balance throughout her body and energy system.

HEALING THE SACRAL CHAKRA

The second chakra is the sacral chakra, located just below the navel. It is the center of creativity, desire, sexual emotion, and sexuality, stimulating the creative life force required for existing in the physical world. Some traditions say that this force is the basis for life itself. This is where we store healthy energy for future use when needed. (This creative life force is not the same as the body's fatty tissue, which can be converted to physical energy.)

LOCATION: Just below the navel

CRYSTAL: Carnelian

COLOR: Orange

FRAGRANCE ASSOCATION: Ylang-ylang

KEYWORDS: Connection to other people, creativity, energy, stamina, innocence, sex, fertility, personal control, relationships, surprise, independence, confidence, joy, negotiation, self-employment, happiness, natural cycles

EMOTIONAL/MENTAL HEALING: The key to the sacral chakra is its ability to store instantly usable energy. It's like a switch, providing energy on demand, and it takes only a little practice or a few crystal chakra treatments to tap into this ready source of inner strength. It makes your creativity flow so you touch everyone around you with your warmth, because that is what happens when you say someone is a "warm person"—it's the energy radiating out from within them that makes them attractive. This brings new relationships, friendships, and opportunity into your life, promoting joy, happiness, and fertility, and dispelling sadness. It can have a profound effect in the treatment of ME, addiction, and eating disorders such as anorexia and bulimia. This added power gives you self-confidence, which helps you to control your emotions.

PHYSICAL HEALING: The energy store is released naturally when the body needs it. This increases stamina and prompts wide-ranging effects throughout the body, so that almost anything from muscle cramps to infections may be relieved. The health of the sacral chakra affects the intestines, spleen, kidneys, and gallbladder. Chronic lower-back pain, sciatica, gynecological problems, disorders around the pelvic girdle, sexual potency, and urinary problems may be the result of an unbalanced chakra. Conception, pregnancy, fetal development, and the health of mother and newborn baby are all enhanced by a healthy sacral chakra. It helps to regulate the menstrual cycle, and when this doesn't happen it shows as cramps, excessive bleeding, an erratic cycle, or PMS (premenstrual syndrome). Working on your sacral chakra can also help allergies, arthritis, and rheumatism. It can strengthen the immune system and aid cleansing and detoxing.

SPIRITUAL HEALING: The energy stored in your sacral chakra, ready for you to draw upon, is not just physical—it can be used for anything. It connects you to your natural cycles and those of the universe, like an innocent child, allowing you to experience living in the moment full of surprise and wonder. Taoism refers to this state as the "uncarved block," as it is possible to make anything from it. Spiritual pursuits such as meditation become easier—many meditations ask you to breathe down into this area of your body. All psychic abilities are enhanced as you connect unimpeded to spirit, God, the universal creative life force, or whatever you believe is out there. The extra energy gives you a sense of peace, bringing calmness to all you do. In the same way, the sacral chakra affects the symbolic digestion of creative ideas and spiritual energy.

LIFESTYLE: Whether it's washing the dishes or running a marathon, if your sacral chakra is in balance and you focus on it, you will find any physical task easier. It facilitates the flow of creative and artistic energies, freeing you to be inspired at

How to Tell if Your Sacral Chakra Is Out of Balance

If the sacral chakra is blocked, energy moves very slowly or doesn't flow at all, leading to a lack of stamina. You can feel lethargic, lonely, and sad. ME (myalgic encephalitis) is a severe problem that may result from an imbalance in the sacral chakra. Imbalance in this chakra is often related to sexual issues, which may arise from imagination or beliefs but can derive from a single incident or repeated experiences. Common symptoms include:

- Chronic lower-back pain
- Sciatica
- Gynecological problems and disorders around the pelvic girdle
- Menstrual cycle dysfunction
- Intestinal disorders
- Spleen conditions
- Kidney and urinary tract infections and disease
- Gallbladder disorders
- Sexual impotence
- Lack of confidence
- Unbalanced emotions
- Eating disorders

home, work, and play. You will notice changes to yourself and to those around you. You affect everything and everyone you touch, and the state of your energy is decisive in these interactions. The old adage that first impressions count is true and a balanced sacral chakra will help you to quickly connect to anyone you meet.

ALTERNATIVE CRYSTALS: Orange calcite, copper, pink banded agate, moonstone, pearl, gray banded agate, vanadinite, chiastolite, crocoite, sardonyx, Picasso marble, halite

HEALING BENEFITS

When the sacral chakra is balanced, you feel energized in every area of your life. You are free to take advantage of opportunities as they arise, so that you move forward, making your decisions as you go. Life seems to flow. Everything you do becomes calmer and easier, allowing you more time and freedom to enjoy whatever the world has to offer.

The sacral chakra represents the creative life force within you.

CRYSTALS FOR THE SACRAL CHAKRA

You can work with crystals to balance and heal the sacral chakra by placing the crystal directly on the energy center on your body (see page 53), by carrying it with you all the time or, if suitable, taping it to your body with surgical tape. You can also try meditating with your chosen crystal and putting it by your bed or under your pillow at night. For more information on these and other healing techniques, refer to Chapter 5.

Carnelian

Orange calcite

Vanadinite

Copper

Crocoite

Moonstone

Chiastolite

Picasso marble

Pink banded agate

Sardonyx

Pearl

Gray banded agate

Halite

CARNELIAN

Variety of chalcedony forming orange pebbles; can also be red, pink, or brown.

Common alternative names: Cornelian, sard

Common sources: Worldwide, especially Brazil, India, Uruguay

Astrological associations: Taurus, Cancer, Leo

Chakra: Sacral

Healing qualities: This "feel better stone" boosts personal power and self-esteem. It gives you both courage and compassion, helping to dispel negative emotions such as anger, envy, fear, rage, sorrow, and jealousy. By bringing focus and balance, it enhances your connection to spirit and inspiration. This leads to confidence and inquisitiveness, beating away confusion, apathy, lethargy, and laziness, and it is helpful in the treatment of ME (myalgic encephalitis) and eating disorders. Carnelian helps you see the links between dis-ease and emotions so you can deal with the emotions and prevent dis-ease. It is good for anyone who undertakes live performance, such as actors and musicians as well as people involved in meditation retreats or study.

Physical benefits: Boosts appetite, vitality, and memory and is good for digestion, the gallbladder, lungs, liver, kidneys, pancreas, spleen, thyroid gland, spine, tissue regeneration, and the voice and speech. Helps asthma, hay fever, bronchitis, neuralgia, the common cold, infection, and liver conditions such as jaundice. Traditionally carnelian is sucked to reduce thirst and is also made into a topical elixir for minor cuts and grazes.

ORANGE CALCITE

Bright to pale orange rocks.

Common source: Mexico

Astrological associations: Cancer, Leo

Chakra: Sacral

Healing qualities: Helps to balance energy, bringing vitality and calm and reducing feelings of aggression and belligerence. Promotes inspiration and creativity. Balances sexuality, enhancing it when needed.

Physical benefits: Calms excessive physical energy, helping to alleviate stress related-symptoms, especially those associated with digestive disorders, such as IBS (irritable bowel syndrome).

COPPER

A metal found in free-form shapes, dendrites, plates, and rhombohedral crystals.

Common source: USA

Astrological associations: Taurus, Sagittarius

Chakra: Sacral

Healing qualities: This "feel better stone" balances emotions and boosts chi, giving vitality and banishing exhaustion, lethargy, and tiredness. This also helps to prevent mood swings and reduce impatience and excitability. In addition, it is a lucky stone.

Physical benefits: Good for the circulation and stimulates the metabolism. Aids detoxing and helps general malaise, infected wounds, and joint conditions such as inflammation, bursitis, arthritis, and rheumatism.

PINK BANDED AGATE

Agate variety with pink, white, and sometimes gray banding and patterns.

Common source: Botswana

Astrological associations: Scorpio, Taurus

Chakras: Sacral, heart

Healing qualities: A very feminine stone that helps both women and men connect to their female side. Promotes femininity, creativity, nurturing, finding solutions to problems, attention to detail, universal love, and seeing the whole picture. Helps to relieve depression and stress.

Physical benefits: Good for the nervous system. Aids detoxing.

MOONSTONE

Variety of feldspar exhibiting chatoyancy. Colors include white, cream, yellow, brown, blue, green, and rainbow (white with a blue color flash).

Common source: India

Astrological associations: Cancer, Libra, Scorpio

Chakra: Sacral

Healing qualities: Helps you get in touch with your inner self, bringing calm, balance, and control to your emotions. Helps healthy energy flow by releasing blocks throughout the energy system. A soothing crystal, promoting compassion, peace of mind, wisdom, sexuality, passion, intuition, insight, creativity, confidence, composure, protection for travelers, good luck, and a happy home. It banishes pessimism and oversensitivity and encourages change and new beginnings, helping and breaking bad cycles and repeated patterns.

Physical benefits: Good for the circulation, pituitary gland, eyes, a youthful appearance, fertility, pregnancy and childbirth, female hormones, menstrual cycle, and menstruation. Helps PMS (premenstrual syndrome), period pains, menopausal symptoms, constipation, water retention, swelling, insect bites, and anaphylactic shock. A topical elixir of moonstone is good for the hair and skin.

PEARL

Formed within the shells of oysters or other mollusks, pearls can be white, black, gray, pinkish, or yellowish.

Common sources: China, Japan

Astrological associations: Cancer, Gemini

Chakra: Sacral

Healing qualities: Promotes emotional control and focuses the mind, benefiting feminine qualities, sexuality, wisdom, fidelity, chastity, and purity. Reduces irritability and antisocial behavior.

Physical benefits: Good for fertility and childbirth, and also for digestion, reducing biliousness, bloating, and discomfort.

GRAY BANDED AGATE

Gray and white banded or patterned variety of agate.

Common source: Botswana

Astrological association: Scorpio

Chakra: Sacral

Healing qualities: Enhances the release of usable stored energy in the sacral chakra, benefiting many conditions on all levels.

Physical benefits: Good for digestion and helps general malaise, reducing fatigue. Helps in the treatment of ME (myalgic encephalitis).

VANADINITE

Barrel-shaped and hollow prismatic crystals and masses.

Common source: Morocco

Astrological association: Virgo

Chakra: Sacral

Healing qualities: Helps the thinking process and goal-setting. Reduces compulsive behavior such as overspending and OCD (obsessive-compulsive disorder). Benefits meditation and reduces exhaustion.

Physical benefits: Good for lungs, improves breathing and breath control, and helps asthma. Also good for bladder.

Caution: NO ELIXIR.

CHIASTOLITE

This variety of andalusite forms fat crystals that exhibit a cross pattern in cross section; may be brown or green with black "cross" markings.

Common alternative names: Cross stone, andalusite

Common source: China

Astrological association: Libra

Chakra: Sacral

Healing qualities: This is traditionally a sign of the Christian Cross and so is associated with its healing energies and with ideas such as love, peace, devotion, understanding the dying process, death, and rebirth, as well as with change and astral travel. It helps creativity, problem-solving, and practicality. Perhaps the phrase "when the going gets tough, the tough get going" is apt to describe this crystal's potential.

Physical benefits: Good for the circulation and for increasing milk production in nursing mothers. Helps to reduce fever and may help chromosome damage.

CROCOITE

Prismatic orange crystals, masses, and aggregates.

Common source: Australia

Astrological association: Aries

Chakra: Sacral

Healing qualities: Eases the distress of change, especially major changes such as divorce (it is known as "the divorce stone"), calming emotions and boosting intuition and creativity. Helps you cope with death or any loss. Balances sexuality.

Physical benefits: Helps disorders of the reproductive system.

Caution: NO ELIXIR.

SARDONYX

Variety of onyx that contains carnelian and shows a combination of black, red, brown, white, and clear bands.

Common source: India

Astrological association: Aries

Chakra: Sacral

Healing qualities: Encourages balance in marriage and other cohabiting relationships, and is also good for socializing. Reduces hesitation, promoting courage. Brings good luck and helps protect against crime.

Physical benefits: Good for strength, muscle development, and all types of sports training.

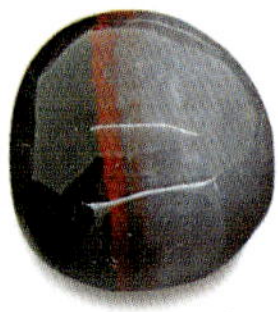

PICASSO MARBLE

Patterned marble in color combinations of black, brown, yellow, and white.

Common alternative names: Picasso stone, Picasso jasper

Common source: USA

Astrological associations: Sagittarius, Cancer

Chakra: Sacral

Healing qualities: Good for creative pursuits such as art and music. A grounding stone, it calms the mind, alleviating unsettled and subconscious thoughts, reducing anxiety, worry, and stress, easing change, and promoting perseverance.

Physical benefits: Good for the circulation, digestion, metabolism, weight loss, and detoxing. Helps carpal tunnel syndrome.

HALITE

Salt crystals, massive or cubic. Colors include orange, green, whitish, yellow, red, purple, blue, and colorless.

Common sources: Australia, France, Germany, Poland, USA

Astrological associations: Cancer, Pisces

Chakra: Sacral

Healing qualities: Boosts endurance and reduces mood swings, bringing a more even balance to life.

Physical benefits: Balances body fluids and helps reduce water retention. Good for small and large intestines.

Caution: NO ELIXIR.

Crystal Clinic

My clients Tom and Sarah had been wanting to have a baby but had been unsuccessful, despite being in a loving relationship. They had seen counselors and doctors, who had been unable to find a physical or psychological reason for the failure to conceive. The couple approached me, as is all too often the case, as a "last resort."

After a long discussion we started a series of treatments, beginning with a general crystal chakra healing for each of them. I noticed that Sarah was very stressed, perhaps through concern about the fertility issue, but I suspected that there was something else she wasn't talking about or didn't even realize.

Their second treatment the following week was enlightening. I focused on the sacral chakra, placing moonstone on the chakra and arranging two pearls and two pink banded agate stones alternately to create a cross around it, interlinked with four mini quartz crystals. Each crystal was energized with my quartz master crystal. The treatments were the same for each of them, but Tom found his treatment calm and relaxing, while Sarah experienced great discomfort and emotional distress—which, although unpleasant for her at the time, was the real start of her healing process. We talked and I discovered that she worked as a complaints manager at a call center. All day long she would deal with only the worst of the complaints, which her staff couldn't deal with. She felt permanently under threat and bereft of energy.

Clearing the sacral chakra allowed Sarah to understand what her issues were. Tom was given a rose quartz pendant to wear to help him cope with his wife's predicted emotional releases.

Sarah had several more weekly treatments before she felt ready to change her job. Soon after this she conceived, and she then worked with chrysocolla and moonstone, placing them on her stomach each evening for 20–30 minutes. Eventually she gave birth to a healthy girl.

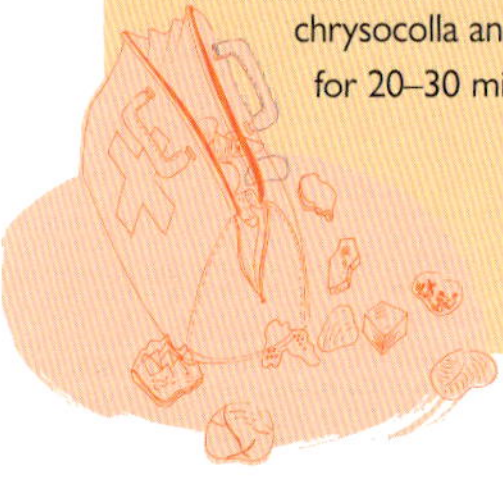

HEALING THE SOLAR PLEXUS CHAKRA

The third chakra is located at the solar plexus, in the middle of the body just below the breastbone. It is the center of personal power, ambition, desire, and emotion. Feelings and the sense of touch are processed through the solar plexus chakra, hence the phrase "gut feeling." Being at the physical center of the body, the solar plexus chakra is the point of "centering," where we come to stillness.

When healthy, this chakra is said to produce a protective and cleansing energy that flows out through the body's energy system, dispersing any negativity held in any of the other chakras. I believe that this is because when the solar plexus chakra is healthy, you become more aware of your own internal energy and how you feel about the world and events around you. This allows you to make continuous subtle adjustments to your internal energy and to your reactions to the outside world. It is also the site of your "internal pendulum," your instinctive "yes/no response" to everything that happens to you (see pages 25–26).

LOCATION: Behind the soft cartilage at bottom of breastbone

CRYSTAL: Citrine

COLOR: Yellow

FRAGRANCE ASSOCIATION: Neroli

KEYWORDS: Bravery, strength, confidence, self-esteem, nurturing, emotions, trust, responsibility for decisions, logic, memory, concentration, learning, adaptability, recovery after surgery

EMOTIONAL/MENTAL HEALING: If your solar plexus chakra is out of balance, you often feel drained. Typical symptoms are lack of concentration, failing memory, falling asleep during the day, and insomnia. It is particularly difficult to meditate, as you will be either nodding off or easily distracted. This chakra is greatly affected by stress, especially what I call "21st-century stress": the idea of attempting to do too much, always running around trying to be in too many places at once and multitasking when you're not dashing around. This leads to a lack of quality time. In fact, it doesn't matter how busy you are if you can focus on each thing you do, but "21st-century stress" makes you unfocused and uncentered. As stress affects the weakest part of the body, imbalance in the solar plexus chakra can be manifested in almost any physical, emotional, psychological, or spiritual symptom throughout the body or its energy system. A healthy third chakra promotes versatility as you learn to adapt from one situation to the next.

PHYSICAL HEALING: Working with crystals on the solar plexus chakra can help digestive disorders, indigestion, food allergies, stomach ulcers, intestinal disorders, gallstones and bile, liver ailments, and eating disorders such as anorexia and bulimia. It promotes the healthy functioning of the lymphatic and nervous systems, enhances healthy metabolism, aids the pancreas and adrenal gland, and helps recovery after surgery. Through its role in balancing blood sugar levels, it helps diabetes. Arthritis, rheumatism, stress-affected skin problems such as eczema, and phobias can all be helped.

SPIRITUAL HEALING: This is the area that puts our beliefs, ideas, thoughts, and creative inspiration into practice and where we act on the concepts of trust and honor. When it is out of balance, either you have ideas and thoughts that go around in your head without your doing anything with them, or you are running around the whole time like a headless chicken with no direction. A balanced third chakra gives your actions purpose.

LIFESTYLE: Because the solar plexus chakra is the crossroads of the physical body, a healthy one has energy flowing through it, linking your whole body. It encourages the development of leadership skills such as bravery, confidence, self-esteem, inner strength, logic, the abilities to lead by example and take responsibility for your own decisions, and emotional control. Your "internal pendulum" (see pages 25–26 and 95) will help you see the truth within other people.

The solar plexus chakra can bring you a sense of stillness.

Alternative crystals: Imperial topaz, amber, tiger's eye, yellow jasper, hessonite, anhydrite, ametrine, beryl, schalenblende, heliodor, sulfur, golden calcite

HEALING BENEFITS

A balanced solar plexus chakra helps give a physical focus to everything you do. The feeling of being centered and still is beneficial to everything but particularly to study and learning new skills. You feel emotion in your heart but it is through this energy hot spot that you act on your emotions. When it's healthy you have self-esteem and self-respect, are less sensitive to criticism, and can care for yourself and nurture others.

How to Tell if Your Solar Plexus Chakra Is Out of Balance

If the solar plexus chakra is blocked, energy moves very slowly or doesn't flow at all, leading to a feeling of being drained and a loss of personal power and self-respect. Problems in the solar plexus chakra are often related to "21st-century stress" (see page 96).

Typical symptoms are:

- Lack of concentration
- Failing memory
- Falling asleep during the day
- Insomnia
- Digestive disorders
- Eating disorders
- Stress-related skin conditions

CRYSTALS FOR THE SOLAR PLEXUS CHAKRA

You can work with crystals to balance and heal the solar plexus chakra by placing the crystal directly on the energy center on your body (see page 53), carrying it with you all the time or, if suitable, taping it to your body with surgical tape. You can also try meditating with your chosen crystal and putting it by your bed or under your pillow at night. For more information on these and other healing techniques, refer to Chapter 5.

Citrine

Ametrine

Beryl

Imperial topaz

Schalenblende

Amber

Tiger's eye

Heliodor

Sulfur

Yellow jasper

Hessonite

Golden calcite

Anhydrite

CITRINE

Variety of quartz in which the yellow, golden, or lemon color is the result of heat from volcanic and other earth activity.

Common source: Brazil

Astrological associations: Gemini, Aries, Libra, Leo

Chakra: Solar plexus

Healing qualities: Keeping a citrine crystal—known as the "money stone"—in your purse, wallet, or pocket brings wealth and abundance, which is not just financial; it's a "feel better stone," bringing abundance on all levels. Citrine helps you make choices and decisions, aids problem-solving, increases awareness and self-esteem, helps you control anger and other unwanted emotions, balances yin and yang energies, and promotes relationships. It boosts energy and creativity and is particularly helpful for teaching, writing, studying, or learning. By helping to eliminate emotional toxins, it leads to the possibility of new beginnings. Citrine is also a wonderful tool when you want to sell your home, as it promotes abundance, making buyers feel welcome and uplifted, and creating the feeling that it would be a nice place to live. Simply place a small crystal or crystal cluster in each room and one large crystal in the entry hall or living room.

Physical benefits: Good for the digestive system, heart, liver, kidneys, thyroid gland, and thymus, helping associated disorders and symptoms such as anemia, jaundice, nausea, vomiting, constipation, and diarrhea. It aids the elimination of toxins and boosts tissue regeneration and recovery after operations. It also improves eyesight and the aura.

IMPERIAL TOPAZ

Golden prismatic crystals and alluvial pebbles.

Common sources: Brazil, USA

Astrological associations: Sagittarius, Leo, Pisces

Chakras: Solar plexus, crown

Healing qualities: Helps to relieve "21st-century stress" (see page 96) and brings a universal connection to everything, giving a feeling of oneness. Promotes mental energy and so is good for thoughts, ideas, creativity, relaxation, and meditation. Also increases physical attraction.

Physical benefits: Aids all stress-related conditions, liver, gallbladder, and hormone balance.

AMBER

Fossilized resin from prehistoric trees that may have inclusions of animal/plant material. Colors include yellow, orange, and brown, plus green (artificial color).

Common sources: Baltic region including Latvia, Lithuania, Poland (copal, or "new amber," comes from Colombia, the Dominican Republic, and Madagascar)

Astrological associations: Leo, Aquarius

Chakra: Solar plexus

Healing qualities: Centuries of tradition surrounding amber suggest its protective qualities. It is worn as a talisman by warriors to bring good luck. Wearing it purifies body, mind, and spirit, and it symbolizes the renewal of marriage vows in a similar way to an eternity ring. Amber is good for the mind, improving memory and reducing absent-mindedness. Because it is calming, it allows the intellect to work, which means that decision-making is easier. Perhaps its greatest quality lies in its ability to help you recognize and fulfill your dreams,

goals, and ideals. It also helps you to balance yin and yang energy, helps remove emotional blocks and negativity, and aids treatment of schizophrenia and recovery from abuse. Amber is sometimes burned as an incense to cleanse spaces and remove negativity, making it perfect for therapy rooms.

Physical benefits: Is helpful in the treatment of bacterial infection and acne. It is also beneficial to the heart, hormone balance, postoperative healing, detoxing, throat, kidneys, and bladder, and can help asthma. Can be applied as an antiseptic topical elixir and is drunk as an elixir to relieve constipation. Its disinfectant qualities meant that in medieval times it was used as a fumigant. Historically, it was chewed by babies to relieve teething discomfort.

TIGER'S EYE

Quartz has replaced asbestos while retaining the fibrous structure of the original asbestos crystal, giving the characteristic chatoyancy shown by the tiger's eye family. Colors include gold, yellow, and brown (commonly all in the same specimen), red, and blue. Color varieties are blue hawk's eye (see page 135) and red falcon's eye (see page 76).

Common source: South Africa

Astrological association: Capricorn

Chakra: Solar plexus

Healing qualities: Brings courage and calmness. It dispels inhibitions, introversion, fear, intolerance, negativity, and prejudice, creating order out of chaos. It is supportive of intuition, balances yin and yang energy, and promotes balance between the right and left hemispheres of the brain. Because it sharpens the mind, it is particularly helpful for investigators such as police, scientists, insurers, and accountants. A "feel better stone," tiger's eye helps to eliminate worry and depression and encourages new beginnings, leading to success and wealth. Being a grounding crystal, it is helpful in distant healing.

Physical benefits: Good for the whole digestive system and helps associated conditions, including flatulence, nausea, and diverticulosis. Can also help treat some eye diseases and bone fractures.

YELLOW JASPER

A yellow variety of opaque chalcedony.

Common source: South Africa

Astrological association: Leo

Chakra: Solar plexus

Healing qualities: Helps intellectual pursuits, such as research and study; provides protection, especially for travelers.

Physical benefits: General tonic for the body that aids digestion and increases energy.

HESSONITE

Brown (from cinnamon to yellowish) form of grossular garnet.

Common alternative name: Cinnamon stone

Common source: Madagascar

Astrological association: Aries

Chakras: Solar plexus, sacral

Healing qualities: A crystal that gives the courage needed for new challenges. Dispels negativity, inferiority complexes, and victim mentality. In meditation, it can help you advance to the next level of awareness.

Physical benefits: Eases flatulence and colic. Good for the olfactory and lymphatic systems and aids detoxing.

ANHYDRITE

Clear, gray, and white tabular crystals and masses.

Common source: Mexico

Astrological associations: Cancer, Pisces, Scorpio

Chakras: Solar plexus, sacral

Healing qualities: Bringing acceptance and aiding the release of past issues, it is helpful for coping with and understanding the dying process.

Physical benefits: Promotes strength and stamina, helps throat conditions, and relieves water retention and swelling.

AMETRINE

Naturally occurring combination of amethyst and citrine, which is purple and gold in color.

Common source: Bolivia

Astrological association: Libra

Chakras: Solar plexus, crown

Healing qualities: Removes physical, mental, emotional, and spiritual blockages, promoting an intellectual understanding of spirituality and allowing you to bring your beliefs into your everyday life and actions. This inspiring crystal is great for creativity and creative pursuits such as art and music. It promotes change, bringing tranquility, removing worry, and reducing prejudice and ignorance. It accelerates the meditation process, so you get to your own deepest state quicker. It also boosts the aura, facilitates astral travel, and balances yin and yang energies.

Physical benefits: Relieves muscle tension. Helps to repair chromosome damage and reduce rejection in organ transplants.

BERYL

Hexagonal prismatic crystals with flat or occasionally small pyramidal terminations. Color varieties include a milky yellowish green, white, red bixbite, and colorless goshenite, as well as yellow to gold heliodor (see page 106), green emerald (see page 120), pink morganite (see page 123), and blue aquamarine (see page 134).

Common sources: Africa, Brazil, Pakistan, Russia

Astrological associations: Gemini, Pisces, Aries, Leo

Chakras: Solar plexus, crown

Healing qualities: Brings emotional balance, helping to eliminate the effects of "21st-century stress," and promotes initiative, wisdom, and adaptability, helping you to fulfill your potential. It is employed in ceremonies to facilitate this.

Physical benefits: Eases belching, aids the nervous system, and is good for the pancreas. Promotes physical activity and vitality.

SCHALENBLENDE

This compact variety of sphalerite is yellow to brown in color, often with silver-gray bands of galena and marcasite.

Common sources: Germany, Poland

Astrological associations: Aquarius, Pisces

Chakra: Solar plexus

Healing qualities: Enhances magic, divination, and mediumship. Gives protection and is helpful for travel and new beginnings.

Physical benefits: Good for the immune system.

HELIODOR

Variety of beryl, from yellow to gold in color.

Common source: Brazil

Astrological association: Leo

Chakras: Solar plexus, crown

Healing qualities: Aids communication, encourages compassion, promotes mental balance. It also provides protection, especially of your family, house, or car when you are away from them.

Physical benefits: Good for the liver, spleen, and pancreas.

SULFUR

Masses, nodules, pyramidal, and tabular crystals.

Common source: Sicily

Astrological association: Leo

Chakra: Solar plexus

Healing qualities: Aids mental balance, inspiration, and reasoning; dispels willfulness.

Physical benefits: Boosts energy and helps insect bites, infection, fibrous tissue growths, painful joints, and swelling. Has also been employed as a fumigant.

Caution: NO ELIXIR.

GOLDEN CALCITE

Rhombohedral and scalenohedral crystals; also found as masses.

Common sources: China, USA

Astrological association: Leo

Chakras: Solar plexus, sacral, crown

Healing qualities: Boosts mental energy, creativity and ideas, banishing self-limiting beliefs. Aids calm communication, reducing the likelihood of arguments. Also helpful for divination, past-life recall, and healing visualizations. An elixir drunk through the day can be very calming.

Physical benefits: Good for physical energy, the circulation, nerves, liver, gallbladder, and endocrine glands. Helps fight infection at its onset.

Crystal Clinic

Amy was suffering from recurring headaches, which were bringing her down and causing lethargy during the day. She had lost interest in everything, and although she had previously had an active social life, she now felt no desire to go out and just fell asleep in front of the TV each evening. She was totally stressed out from her multitasking lifestyle.

I gave her one complete crystal chakra healing treatment and asked her to work with imperial topaz for two weeks, keeping it with her all the time, and meditating with it for half an hour each morning and before she went to bed at night. After two weeks she reported that she felt refreshed and had found a new purpose in her life. She'd started a new relationship and said she was going to mount the imperial topaz crystal into a pendant so she could wear it and show it off to all her friends and colleagues.

HEALING THE HEART CHAKRA

Located in the middle of the chest, the fourth chakra is the center of love and compassion. It relates to your connection to everyone and everything around you.

Spirituality, in the sense of "a connection to everything," is the key concept of love. Without this connection we are unable to share the love we all have inside us. This energy hot spot is the deepest point inside us, where the outside world meets our inner being. With each breath we take, we inhale part of the outside world and exchange energy with it, through the physical process of gaseous exchange in the lungs. With this comes a sense of connection with our environment. When we exhale, we share our own internal energy with the space and people around us. This connection is the motor that sends love through the energy system, resulting, for example, in a bridge between the analytical mind and the feeling heart.

LOCATION: Center of the chest

CRYSTAL: Malachite

COLOR: Green

FRAGRANCE ASSOCIATION: Rose

KEYWORDS: Love, safety, trust, adventure, relationships, faithfulness, commitment, forgiveness, compassion, hope, seeing beauty, harmony, kindness, sleep, gentleness

EMOTIONAL/MENTAL HEALING: When the heart chakra is out of balance, we lose touch with our emotions, relationships of all kinds suffer, and we become detached from the world around us. As we slowly become more and more insular, we lock away not only our feelings as we express them but our inner truth—our soul or spirit. We retreat into our head, which creates confusion, a "fog in the mind," blocking mental activities. We stop expressing ourselves, and both vocal and creative expression become duller. We lack energy and can feel constantly drained. We stop advancing on our life path, whether planned by us or by fate, traveling on an ever-decreasing cycle from which there seems no escape. Almost any physical symptoms can develop, which, of course, bring us down further until we lose hope.

A healthy heart chakra allows you to connect to the world around you.

PHYSICAL HEALING: Benefits the chest, heart, and lungs and treats associated ailments and conditions, such as asthma, pneumonia, some allergies, breast, upper back, and shoulder problems, colds, influenza, fevers, ulcers, and stress-related illnesses. Good for breast tissue and cell growth, and general body regeneration, and reduces signs of aging.

SPIRITUAL HEALING: Supports not just physical love between people but a spiritual love of life itself. This is the energy that makes a relationship special, that keeps you up talking all night and gives you extra sparkle. It offers a deeper connection to your loved one and everyone else you meet and bestows a love of life. You can empathize with the suffering of others, and you can enjoy their success and happiness without jealousy or fear of your own inadequacies. All fear stems from this energy center. When we encounter something that makes us fearful, it is because of a stagnation of energy in this chakra, which in turn pushes down to the solar plexus giving that sinking feeling of your internal pendulum (see pages 25–26).

LIFESTYLE: A balanced heart chakra allows you to share with other people. It encourages openness, which others will reflect back to you, like mirrors. All your relationships will benefit, whether partner, relatives, friends, or pets. The world will open for you, creating new opportunities, and you will feel the universe flowing around you. You can enjoy new adventures

Rose quartz can help dispel envy.

without fear but with a new sense of security and trust.

ALTERNATIVE CRYSTALS: Aventurine, rose quartz, garnet, ruby, green moss agate, amazonite, chrysocolla, emerald, jade, peridot, unakite, morganite, rhodochrosite, larimar

HEALING BENEFITS

The heart chakra is the key energy center in the body, the connection between the lower three chakras and the higher three. It is where thoughts are turned into actions and where your feelings are processed. It is the seat of your soul or spirit, your inner self, the bit inside you that connects you to everything around you.

If, as many religions suggest, God is within each of us, then the heart chakra is where He resides. This helps you to see the beauty in everyone and everything, leading to a state of harmony, kindness, gentleness, and peace.

How to Tell if Your Heart Chakra Is Out of Balance

An imbalance in the heart center is linked to an inability to share love, to selfishness, and to feelings of detachment. The heart chakra relates to connection, and when it is blocked, energy moves very slowly or doesn't flow at all, leading to a feeling of disconnection with people, yourself, and life in general. Common symptoms include:

- Emotional confusion
- Unloving and uncaring attitude
- Narrow-mindedness
- Relationship breakdown
- Heart disease
- Chest, lung, and respiratory disorders, such as asthma, and repeated cold and influenza infections
- Early physical signs of aging
- Apparently unrelated symptoms following one after the other

CRYSTALS FOR THE HEART CHAKRA

You can work with crystals to balance and heal the heart chakra by placing the crystal directly on the energy center on your body (see page 53), carrying it with you all the time or, if suitable, taping it to your body with surgical tape. You can also try meditating with your chosen crystal and putting it by your bed or under your pillow at night. For more information on these and other healing techniques, refer to Chapter 5.

Malachite

Emerald

Aventurine

Jade

Peridot

Garnet

Unakite

Ruby

Green moss agate

Rhodochrosite

Amazonite

Larimar

Rose quartz

Morganite

Chrysocolla

MALACHITE

Crystalline aggregates, druses, botryoidal structures, and clusters of radiating fibrous crystals. Single prismatic crystals are rare. More common are malachite pseudomorphs of azurite, which produce a more tabby crystal. Color is green, often with bands in various shades of green and black.

Common sources: Democratic Republic of Congo, USA

Astrological associations: Capricorn, Scorpio

Chakra: Heart

Healing qualities: Promoting emotional balance, bringing calm, and relieving all forms of depression, malachite helps remove unnecessary worry. It is excellent in the treatment of insomnia, and it facilitates dream interpretation and meditation.

Physical benefits: Good for immune system, heart, lungs, pancreas, spleen, pituitary gland, eyesight, and teeth, as well as tissue regeneration, physical balance, endurance, and detoxing. Eases childbirth and helps asthma, epilepsy, tumors, arthritis and rheumatism, inflammation and swelling, bone fractures, and torn muscles. A traditional remedy for cholera.

AVENTURINE

Quartz variety with inclusions of mica, giving a speckled or sparkly effect. Commonly green; other colors include blue, white, reddish peach, and brown.

Common sources: Brazil, India

Astrological association: Aries

Chakra: Heart

Healing qualities: A very calming crystal that protects and soothes the emotions, promoting relaxation. It sponsors creativity, motivation, effective decision-making, and leadership qualities. It also balances yin and yang energies, helps access spirit guides, and protects from "energy vampires" (people who drain others of energy). It is particularly helpful for reducing exam-related stress.

Physical benefits: Benefits muscles, helping muscle injuries such as tears, sprains, and strains. Good for reaction speed, adrenal glands, lungs, and heart, and the urogenital organs. In combination with hawk's eye (see page 135), it eases diarrhea.

ROSE QUARTZ

Pink crystalline masses and, rarely, hexagonal crystals.

Common sources: Brazil, India, Madagascar, South Africa

Astrological associations: Taurus, Libra

Chakra: Heart

Healing qualities: Known as the "love stone," it promotes love on all levels—in relationships, romance, female energy and qualities, and sexual liberation, reducing frustration. It is like a bubble bath for the emotions, easing feelings of anger, fear, guilt, grief, inadequacy, jealousy, and resentment and reducing associated stress, tension, and phobias. Its calming qualities help in any crisis. Generally good for the emotions, it soothes upsets, emotional wounds (the *feeling* of being wounded), and bad memories from childhood experiences, thereby encouraging forgiveness. It also promotes imagination and creativity, such as in art, music, and writing.

Physical benefits: Balances sex drive, fertility, and menstrual cycle, easing PMS (premenstrual syndrome), excess bleeding, and cramps. Encourages a healthy complexion and youthful appearance and reduces wrinkles. Benefits the circulation, spleen, and adrenal glands and can help asthma, heart conditions, kidney disorders (promoting detoxing), general aches and pains, varicose veins, coughs, influenza, burns, sunburn, and vertigo. The rare rose quartz crystals enhance all these qualities.

GARNET

Dodecahedral and trapezohedral crystals and combinations, masses, and layered "plates." Colors include red, pink eudialyte, pinkish red rhodolite, green grossularite, emerald green uvarovite, black melanite, orange spessartine, purply red almandine, yellow-green andradite, yellow and brown hessonite (see page 103).

Common sources: India, Russia, USA

Astrological associations: Leo, Virgo, Capricorn, Aquarius

Chakra: Heart

Healing qualities: Promotes courage and emotional balance, allowing change to happen. Its creative energy draws abundance, increases awareness, and supports magic and spiritual devotion. Life flows better as chaos and disruption disappear. It helps relieve depression and emotional trauma and it benefits the aura.

Physical benefits: Good for the circulation and vitality, and also detoxing. Helps anemia, low blood pressure, and conditions requiring repair and regeneration of tissues. Benefits the spine and spinal fluid, bones, heart, and lungs, and balances sex drive. Can help arthritis, rheumatism, and an underactive thyroid gland. Vitamin and mineral deficiencies such as iodine, calcium, magnesium, and vitamins A, D, and E can also be helped.

RUBY

Red variety of corundum forming tabular crystals.

Common sources: India, Madagascar, Myanmar (Burma), Thailand

Astrological associations: Leo, Scorpio, Cancer, Sagittarius

Chakra: Heart

Healing qualities: Promotes spiritual wisdom so you can see the path to health on all levels—wealth, knowledge, balance, and abundance. It enhances the will to live, the survival mechanism, and the fight-or-flight response, providing protection. The will to live gives us passion and a creative impulse to make decisions and changes that will banish distress and suffering from our lives, and so ruby is good for mental balance, new beginnings and rebirth. It enhances the dream state, facilitates dream interpretation, and helps prevent nightmares. Beneficial for meditation, it speeds attainment of the peak experience (bliss or connection). It aids contact and understanding with spirit guides and distant healing (see page 196–197). Carrying a ruby crystal or placing one in your home is said to give protection from lightning strikes.

Physical benefits: Good for heart and circulation, detoxing, physical energy, immune system, longevity, and brain activity. Helps low blood pressure, anemia, and fever. Benefits the menstrual cycle, menstruation, and associated blood loss, Encourages the healthy development of the embryo in the womb. Record keeper ruby crystals aid access to the Akashic records and facilitate astral travel and remote viewing. Star ruby crystals (showing asterism) bring enlightenment and help energy-cleansing and focus.

GREEN MOSS AGATE

Transparent or translucent green, white, and clear mosslike patterned masses.

Common source: India

Astrological association: Virgo

Chakra: Heart

Healing qualities: Releases trapped emotions, relieving symptoms of anxiety, stress, and tension. Supports acquisition of wealth. Helpful for plant healing and encourages growth of new crops.

Physical benefits: Cleanses the immune system, especially after infection, and eases cold and influenza symptoms. Good for digestion and for eyes. Can help dehydration and fungal infections, and can be applied as a topical elixir to treat skin disorders.

AMAZONITE

Green, usually opaque variety of microcline (variety of feldspar), forming crystals and masses. Color varies from yellow-green to blue-green.

Common alternative names: Amazon jade, Amazon stone

Common sources: Brazil, Russia, USA

Astrological association: Virgo

Chakra: Heart

Healing qualities: A "feel better stone" that calms and soothes nerves and a troubled mind. It reduces stress, boosts the aura and creativity, and can help in the treatment of mental disorders such as schizophrenia.

Physical benefits: Good for the nervous system and heart.

CHRYSOCOLLA

Forms layers, masses, botryoidal structures, and druses.

Common sources: Peru, USA

Astrological associations: Gemini, Virgo, Taurus

Chakra: Heart

Healing qualities: Helps heal the emotional heartache of a "broken heart" by releasing negative emotions such as guilt. A "feel better stone," it promotes creativity and female sexuality, helping you let go of tension, phobias, and stressful situations. When you feel better about yourself, you feel no need for gossip. It promotes earth healing and helps revitalize relationships.

Physical benefits: Good for digestion, joints (helping arthritis and rheumatism), metabolism, thyroid gland, and menstrual cycle. Reduces period pains and helps PMS (premenstrual syndrome). Improves oxidation of the blood, which can ease breathing and increase lung capacity, and helps lung conditions such as asthma, bronchitis, emphysema, and TB. It helps to prevent ulcers and aids the treatment of stress-related conditions. During pregnancy it promotes healthy development of the fetus. In the pancreas it supports insulin production and so helps control blood-sugar levels and diabetes. Benefits muscles and helps prevent muscle cramps, especially in the arms and legs. Helps restless leg syndrome and also high blood pressure. Drusy chrysocolla speeds the effects of any other crystal.

EMERALD

Green gem variety of beryl.

Common sources: Colombia for gem quality, Brazil for commercial grade

Astrological associations: Taurus, Gemini, Aries

Chakra: Heart

Healing qualities: Helps to heal the emotional heart, replacing jealousy, dishonesty, and bad temper with honesty and patience.

Physical benefits: Helps asthma. Good for vitality, growth, bones and teeth, fertility, eyesight, and balance. Benefits heart, helping angina and high blood pressure. Boosts immune system, fighting bacterial and viral infections and helping inflammation, sores, and insect bites. Benefits kidneys, liver, and bile ducts, helping jaundice and biliousness, and, I almost forgot, aids memory.

JADE

Masses that are commonly green but can include orange, brown, blue, cream, white, lavender, red, gray, or black. Types of jade include jadeite and nephrite. (Note that "new jade" is actually bowenite.)

Common sources: Canada, China, Myanmar (Burma), USA

Astrological associations: Aries, Gemini, Taurus, Libra

Chakra: Heart

Healing qualities: Brings emotional balance and grounding, boosting confidence and courage, and giving a sense of justice, modesty, and compassion. It removes negativity and is helpful in the treatment of mental disorders such as schizophrenia. When placed under your pillow, jade promotes nighttime dreaming and dream recall. It also

encourages dreams, goals, and ideals in life, offers inner and outer peace, assists problem-solving, and gives protection, especially from accidents. It provides a connection to the wisdom of ancient civilizations and offers shamanic access to spirit worlds.

Physical benefits: Helps asthma, bacterial and viral infections, high blood pressure, eye disorders, and general malaise. It can assist the heart, immune system (especially the lymphatic system), kidneys, gallbladder, spleen, and bladder, as well as the bones, joints, and muscles, and balance. It is good for the female reproductive system, including the menstrual cycle and fertility, and can help period pains and PMS (premenstrual syndrome). A jade elixir can benefit hair and skin and help skin conditions such as acne. It is said to promote longevity.

PERIDOT

Small green prismatic crystals and masses.

Common alternative names: Chrysolite, olivine

Common sources: Afghanistan, Brazil, Canary Islands, Pakistan, Russia, Sri Lanka, USA

Astrological associations: Virgo, Leo, Scorpio, Sagittarius

Chakra: Heart

Healing qualities: A "feel better stone" that offers protection from outside influences, reducing stress and removing the need for ego, anger, and jealousy. It releases emotional blockages, eliminating addictions, especially alcoholism, and negative repeated cycles and behavior patterns. It combats depression by taking away lethargy and laziness and is beneficial for mental health and healing. Helps you reach enlightenment through meditation.

Physical benefits: The cells surrounding all cancers become acidic, and because peridot balances acidity it is the primary crystal recommended for all cancer treatments—always in combination with other crystals beneficial to the affected areas. It is a general physical tonic for the body. Has been known to stimulate birthing contractions. It is good for the digestive system and so helps gastroenteritis, Crohn's disease, IBS (irritable bowel syndrome), and ulcers. It can support weight gain and so helps eating disorders such as anorexia and bulimia. It benefits the gallbladder, liver, pancreas, spleen, heart, and lungs, is good for detoxing, and helps sunburn, astigmatism, and near-sightedness.

UNAKITE

Mixture of epidote, feldspar, and quartz.

Common source: South Africa

Astrological association: Scorpio

Chakra: Heart

Healing qualities: Works on the heart center, relieving grief—especially for the loss of an idea, dream, or goal, whether or not associated with the loss of a loved one. It connects the base and heart chakras, "allowing you to move forward from your heart," removing blocks you put in your own way, letting go of unsettling past experiences and trapped emotions, and allowing you to be in the present moment. It also helps to balance yin and yang energies and aids past-life recall and understanding the causes of dis-ease.

Physical benefits: Good for weight gain. Associated with fertility and the healthy development of the fetus.

MORGANITE

Pink variety of beryl.

Common sources: Brazil, Pakistan

Astrological association: Libra

Chakra: Heart

Healing qualities: Fills the space left in the heart by loss, such as a broken relationship or death. It promotes love and calms the mind, leading to clearer thoughts and allowing you to see things from a different perspective. This brings wisdom, which helps to remove prejudices such as racism and sexism. It promotes contact with spirit guides, aids meditation, and creates a sense of sacredness during rituals. Working with morganite can help improve time management.

Physical benefits: Good for all physical healing. It is especially helpful for chest conditions such as asthma, emphysema, and TB, and it improves oxygenation of the blood.

RHODOCHROSITE

Masses, druses, botryoidal structures, and rare small rhombohedral crystals. The color ranges from pale pink through deep red, yellow, and orange to brown. The massive material commonly has pink and white banding when polished.

Common source: Argentina

Astrological associations: Scorpio, Leo

Chakra: Heart

Healing qualities: Eases "21st-century stress" and emotional trauma, making life flow better, giving courage, and improving memory, thus relieving or preventing a nervous breakdown. Balances yin and yang energies, increasing passion and promoting sex. Supports creative pursuits such as art and music.

Physical benefits: Good for the circulation, heart, kidneys, and spleen, and also combats signs of aging. Helps ME (myalgic encephalitis) and also promotes the healthy development of infants.

LARIMAR

Massive variety of pectolite often found in radial groupings. Colors include blue, green, gray, and red, all possibly with white.

Common alternative name: Pectolite

Common source: Dominican Republic

Astrological association: Leo

Chakra: Heart

Healing qualities: Emanating a soft, gentle healing energy, its soothing vibration helps you to see who you really are. It removes guilt, aggression, and an addiction to materialism, and it facilitates earth healing.

Physical benefits: Good for cartilage, hair, and feet.

Crystal Clinic

Jan, a 28-year-old woman, was brought to see me by her mother. She suffered from asthma, but her mother was more concerned that she had no friends, didn't really do anything, and seemed depressed. She was also prone to catching whatever bug was going around at the time.

I began a standard crystal chakra healing treatment, but as I worked over the heart chakra Jan let out several sighs—an indication that a blockage in the energy flow is being released. When the treatment was concluded, I gave her a large rose quartz crystal to keep with her.

The following week I worked only on the heart center for the whole treatment. I also placed chakra crystals on the other energy centers, but only to hold them in whatever state of balance they were already in. After placing malachite on the heart surrounded by a quartz star interspersed with four more malachite stones, I held my pendulum over Jan's heart and watched. Slowly it began to vibrate in my hand. Then it started to move in a counterclockwise circle, which suggested that it was drawing energy out. After a while I sensed that something was happening in the aura. With the side of my quartz master crystal, I gently combed the aura over the heart chakra, at which point a single tiny tear trickled down her cheek. After the treatment, I gave her malachite and asked her to place it under her pillow that night.

When Jan arrived the next day, she immediately started talking, explaining that ever since her father died six years previously, she had felt she couldn't grieve, because she didn't want to upset her mother. Jan had become more insular and developed asthma. She couldn't accept the love she was being offered because she had blocked her grief for her father. In fact, this was the first time she had even told anyone her father had died.

I gave Jan a crystal chakra set and explained how to place the crystals on her chakras, telling her to do a self-healing treatment each night. Over the next few months, she contacted her old friends and met new ones, felt generally better, went back to work, and didn't have to use her inhaler several times each day.

HEALING THE THROAT CHAKRA

The fifth chakra, located in the middle of the neck above the collarbone, is the center of communication and creative expression. It relates not only to verbal communication, but also to physical communication (body language) and mental contact (telepathy). It's the energy hot spot that tells the world how we are feeling and allows us to "talk our talk," express our beliefs, and share the teaching we each have to give.

LOCATION: Center of the throat

CRYSTAL: Blue lace agate

COLOR: Blue

FRAGRANCE ASSOCIATION: Lavender

KEYWORDS: Communication, expression, responsibility, freedom, choice, willpower, following dreams, creation, addiction, justice, faith, knowledge, ability to make decisions, leadership

EMOTIONAL/MENTAL HEALING: When the throat chakra is out of balance we can lose focus easily. This is commonly identified in children as attention deficit disorders, often linked with hyperactivity, but is found in many adults, too. It is the lack of concentration, the need always to be doing something, and the inability to relax. Emotional trauma can have a severe effect on the health of the throat chakra, leading to a blockage and, in extreme cases, an inability to express any emotion at all. The brain's reasoning processes can be obstructed. This leads to inhibitions in almost any area of life, causing feelings of unease, nervousness, anxiety, and panic attacks. It can even make you believe you are under "psychic attack" from others. All this may in turn lead to a variety of speech impediments.

PHYSICAL HEALING: Working on the throat chakra can benefit the nose, sinuses, throat, tonsils, esophagus, eustachian tubes and related aural problems, hearing, jaws, teeth and gums, mouth, tongue, neck, nervous system, physical trauma such as whiplash, spine, and thyroid gland. It can also help skin rashes, especially in children or when linked to frustration or emotions, and stammering. Common symptoms of throat chakra dysfunction include sore throat, loss of voice, laryngitis, inflammatory disorders of the pharynx, tonsillitis, overactive or underactive thyroid gland, mouth ulcers, teeth and gum conditions, headaches, and ear infections.

SPIRITUAL HEALING: The throat chakra is strongly linked to communication, but this is not just in the physical world. Communicating with spirits, the universal source, God, or whatever you want to call what you personally feel is out there,

The throat chakra represents all forms of communication.

is a fundamental aspect of a healthy throat chakra. Ideals, a sense of justice, sacred knowledge, and wisdom all come from this contact, whether conscious or not. Sometimes an idea just seems to pop into your head, but only if your throat chakra is healthy does it express itself.

LIFESTYLE: A balanced throat chakra full of healthy, flowing energy can help to advance your career, improve communication on all levels, strengthen leadership skills, and develop a strong and sustained marriage or partnership. It can particularly help actors, singers, teachers, and anyone who depends on effective communication and the ability to pass on experience through teaching others. Both our communication with the outside world and how it is reflected back to us are important. This cycle affects how others communicate with us and how we communicate with the outside world.

ALTERNATIVE CRYSTALS: Apatite, turquoise, kyanite, angelite, hemimorphite, aquamarine, hawk's eye, blue chalcedony, aqua aura, cobaltoan calcite, blue quartz, azurite, blue opal, blue fluorite

HEALING BENEFITS

Communication is one of the keys to life, affecting everything we do. Our communication with the world around us is reflected back to us, determining how others communicate with us. Speech is one of the things that makes us uniquely human, allowing us greater expression than all other animals. It comes with a responsibility to be truthful to ourselves and others, and brings freedom of being, mind, intellect, and emotions.

The throat chakra is associated with communication. If it is out of balance and energy flows very slowly or not at all, communication becomes less meaningful and insubstantial. This can lead, in time, to the development of stress-related conditions, from skin rashes to heart attacks, and from a bad back to digestive problems like IBS or Crohn's disease. The lack of communication may have been the result of force of habit through upbringing, or may stem from a single traumatic incident, either known or locked deep in the subconscious. Either way, balancing and healing the throat chakra can help to alleviate both communication issues and many stress-related conditions. It can lead to a happier life, full of self-expression and freedom, which will allow you to cope better with all types of responsibility.

How to Tell if Your Throat Chakra Is Out of Balance

If the throat chakra is blocked, then energy moves very slowly or doesn't flow at all, leading to inadequate self-expression. Poor communication can eventually lead to the development of many stress-related conditions, including the following:

- Skin rashes
- Heart attack
- A weak or bad back
- Digestive problems, such as IBS (irritable bowel syndrome) or Crohn's disease
- Fear of speaking your mind
- Lack of concentration
- Attention defict disorders
- Feelings of unease, nervousness, and anxiety

CRYSTALS FOR THE THROAT CHAKRA

You can work with crystals to balance and heal the throat chakra by placing the crystal directly on the energy center on your body (see page 53), carrying it with you all the time or, if suitable, taping it to your body with surgical tape. You can also try meditating with your chosen crystal and putting it by your bed or under your pillow at night. For more information on these and other healing techniques, refer to Chapter 5.

Blue lace agate

Blue chalcedony

Apatite

Aqua aura

Turquoise

Cobaltoan calcite

Kyanite

Blue quartz

Angelite

Azurite

Hemimorphite

Blue opal

Aquamarine

Blue fluorite

Hawk's eye

BLUE LACE AGATE

Pale blue and white banded variety of agate.

Common source: South Africa

Astrological association: Pisces

Chakra: Throat

Healing qualities: Very gentle and calming, providing balance and emotional stability. It raises your spiritual level and improves communication on all levels, but especially of spiritual ideas. It can increase the power of attunement to spiritual energies such as Reiki.

Physical benefits: Good for eyesight, speech, nails, and the pancreas. Helps stammering, arthritis, fluid retention, trapped nerves, skin growths, and bone fractures. Made into an elixir, it soothes tired eyes.

APATITE

Yellow, green, blue, gray, white, purple, brown, or red-brown prismatic crystals and masses.

Common sources: Canada, Pakistan

Astrological association: Gemini

Chakra: Throat

Healing qualities: Boosts creativity and its expression and calms the throat chakra, leading to clear communication—it is good for communicators of any kind, including healers, teachers, trainers, journalists and writers, publishers, presenters, and performers such as actors and singers. It promotes the intellect and clears mental confusion, allowing you to see the truth. It stops aloofness and negativity. Good for endings, marking a "full stop" after an undesirable chain of events. It balances all the chakras and promotes all psychic abilities, past-life recall, and meditation, leading to a better understanding of your inner self. It balances yin and yang energies.

Physical benefits: Drunk as an elixir, it focuses healing energy on the appropriate body area and is excellent for tissue regeneration and repair. It aids weight loss, acting as an appetite suppressant, and also helps arthritis.

TURQUOISE

Blue, green, or turquoise masses, crusts, and, rarely, small, short, prismatic crystals.

Common sources: China, Myanmar (Burma), USA

Astrological associations: Sagittarius, Pisces, Scorpio

Chakra: Throat

Healing qualities: Aids communication, especially in public speaking and creative expression. Gives protection to travelers (a journey can be anything from a trip around the world to a walk to the grocery store) and is good for travel and air sickness. It brings spirituality, courage, and emotional balance, enhancing friendships, love, and romance. In meditation it grounds peak experiences, enhancing spirit contact, all psychic abilities, and wisdom, and brings mental and spiritual clarity to see your own path and "walk your walk." It helps you to see the beauty in everything, bringing peace of mind and compassion while removing negativity and suspicion. It protects property, helps prevent accidents, balances yin and yang energy, and encourages writing and astral travel.

Physical benefits: Multipurpose healer that is good for the circulation, lungs, throat, muscles, tissue regeneration, weight gain, detoxing, and postoperative recovery. It aids absorption of nutrients and helps general malaise, headaches, backache, whiplash injury, arthritis, rheumatism, asthma, bronchitis, influenza, allergies, conditions caused by pollutants, cataracts, wounds, and discomfort from gas. As an elixir, it benefits stress-related skin disorders.

KYANITE

Blade-type crystals, fibers, and masses. Colors include blue, black, gray, white, green, yellow, and pink.

Common source: Brazil

Astrological associations: Taurus, Libra, Aries

Chakra: Throat

Healing qualities: An excellent aid to communication, it helps you "talk your talk." It can align all the chakras, releasing energy blocks to bring tranquility, calm, perseverance, and reason, and create the perfect internal space for getting started with meditation. It aids connection to spirit guides and promotes dream recall and understanding, attunements, and sacred ceremony. It increases both mental stamina and psychic awareness and it helps to balance yin and yang energy.

Physical benefits: Good for the throat and improves vocal quality, so is especially useful for your singing voice. Benefits muscles, urological system, all glands, and brain.

ANGELITE

Blue/white nodules and masses.

Common source: Peru

Astrological association: Aquarius

Chakra: Throat

Healing qualities: Creates a feeling of security, giving comfort in grief. It balances emotional wobbles, reducing anger. It increases awareness and communication on all levels, including spirit, channeling, and telepathy, helping you to connect to your angels, guardians, and totem animals; it makes astral travel and rebirthing easier. Encourages psychic and spiritual healing and provides protection on these levels when it is drunk as an elixir. It is also good for people who work with numbers, such as accountants.

Physical benefits: Good for blood vessels and hemoglobin production, and it is useful in fighting infectious diseases. Benefits throat, thymus, and all five physical senses. Applied as a topical elixir, it makes an effective insect repellent.

HEMIMORPHITE

Various masses, including "fans" and botryoidal formations, and tabular crystals—blue, green, gray, white, and colorless.

Common source: China

Astrological association: Libra

Chakra: Throat

Healing qualities: A "feel better stone" boosting self-confidence and creativity, making you feel lucky, and helping to maintain health. It banishes ego, selfishness, and anger.

Physical benefits: Good for the blood. Helps ulcers, poisoning, pain, vomiting, and venereal diseases. Benefits dieting and weight loss.

AQUAMARINE

Blue-green variety of beryl.

Common sources: Afghanistan, Brazil, Namibia, Pakistan, USA

Astrological associations: Gemini, Pisces, Aries

Chakra: Throat

Healing qualities: Relieves stress by giving courage, bringing calm, and aiding peaceful, clear communication. Stimulates the brain, boosting intellect and learning. It gently washes away blocks in chakras to enhance energy flow. A centering crystal, it is excellent for meditation as it aids spiritual awareness and development, exploring the truth about your inner self and your higher self. As well as encouraging you to take

responsibility for your own actions, it promotes compassion and tolerance and dispels judgmental attitudes. It also protects travelers.

Physical benefits: Promotes healthy teeth. Good for lymph, blood, and other body fluids, mucous membranes, eyes and eyesight, and kidneys. Helps water retention, swollen glands, and swelling. It is cooling in hot climates. Visualization with aquamarine can help conditions caused by pollutants.

HAWK'S EYE

Blue variety of tiger's eye.

Common alternative name: Blue tiger's eye

Common source: South Africa

Astrological association: Capricorn

Chakras: Throat, brow

Healing qualities: Brings focus, combating disarray and boosting psychic abilities.

Physical benefits: Good for the throat, pharynx, and larynx. Benefits peristalsis in digestion and, when combined with aventurine, helps diarrhea.

BLUE CHALCEDONY

Light blue variety of chalcedony.

Common source: South Africa

Astrological associations: Cancer, Sagittarius

Chakra: Throat

Healing qualities: Excellent for dealing with childhood issues as it eases communication and promotes emotional expression. It helps in the treatment of alcoholism and is good for letting go of "stuff," losing the need to surround yourself with material things.

Physical benefits: Good for weight loss.

AQUA AURA

Quartz crystal bonded with gold, giving beautiful, mostly clear blue crystals and clusters.

Common source: USA

Astrological association: Leo

Chakras: Throat, brow

Healing qualities: Boosts the aura, giving protection, and enhancing all psychic abilities. A "feel better stone," it dispels negativity and depression and eases sadness, loss, and grief. It is very good for treating shock and emotional trauma.

Physical benefits: Benefits throat and helps physical trauma, such as whiplash, headaches, and tension in the neck and shoulders.

COBALTOAN CALCITE

Drusy crusts, spherical masses, and, rarely, crystals often found with, or near, malachite.

Common alternative name: Cobaltocalcite

Common sources: Democratic Republic of Congo, Morocco

Astrological association: Cancer

Chakras: Throat, heart, brow, crown

Healing qualities: Encourages you to see the beauty in everyone, every thing, and in every situation you encounter. Helps you learn each lesson on your path to finding your inner truth and life purpose. It draws out inner hurts and emotional pain, allowing the expression of emotions and attracting your desires.

Physical benefits: Helps all stress-related conditions.

BLUE QUARTZ

Clear or white quartz with blue tourmaline (indicolite) inclusions. Note that there are several other minerals called "blue quartz," which are not included here.

Common source: Minas Gerais, Brazil (only current source)

Astrological associations: Libra, Taurus

Chakra: Throat

Healing qualities: Enhances the connection to those around you, the universe, spirit, and God, giving a sense of bliss. Aids communication on all planes and helps you to express what's in your mind. It brings "stuff" such as issues, thoughts, judgmental attitudes, and "isms" to the surface, allowing them to clear while keeping you grounded, easing the energy shift often associated with healing. Brings a sense of well-being, emotional balance, and happiness. While promoting awareness, self-reliance, and spontaneity, it dispels anger, introversion, apprehension, and anxiety. Good for telepathy, it gives deeper insight into all forms of divination, such as tarot card readings.

Physical benefits: Good for the spleen, endocrine system, blood, and metabolism, boosting vitality.

AZURITE

Masses, nodules, and, rarely, tabular and prismatic crystals of azure or paler blues.

Common alternative name: Blue malachite

Common sources: China, Morocco, USA

Astrological association: Sagittarius

Chakra: Throat

Healing qualities: Known as the "Stone of Heaven," it enhances creativity and psychic abilities, promotes compassion and empathy, and helps you to express feelings, thoughts, and psychic information.

Physical benefits: Good for blood and the nervous system, and helps arthritis.

BLUE OPAL

Blue masses sometimes showing iridescence.

Common alternative name: Andean opal

Common sources: Canada, Peru

Astrological associations: Cancer, Taurus

Chakra: Throat

Healing qualities: Promotes communication, the courage to speak your mind, and connection with other people, as well as boosting problem-solving skills and creativity. It is known as the "stone of thieves" as it bestows invisibility.

Physical benefits: Aids metabolism and iron balance, relieving anemia and fatigue. Helps prevent hair loss.

BLUE FLUORITE

A blue variety of fluorite forming cubic or octahedral crystals.

Common source: China

Astrological associations: Capricorn, Pisces

Chakra: Throat

Healing qualities: Is calming for the emotions and improves communication with spirit.

Physical benefits: Good for tear ducts, mucous membranes, nose, inner ear, balance, throat, and speech.

Crystal Clinic

Rosalie arrived wearing a neck brace which she had had for eight weeks, since having a car accident. She was suffering from whiplash. I explained that although whiplash often causes some minor physical injury, it is rare to suffer any serious damage. (However, this can sometimes occur, so always consult a doctor to make sure that there is no major damage, especially to the spine.) I told her that it was much more likely to have caused a severe energetic "bump" resulting in the throat chakra being knocked out of alignment.

There were many other minor symptoms and issues arising from the accident and from her having to wear the neck brace for so long. She also explained that she often became nervous for no obvious reason and found it difficult to express her feelings. I placed the crystal chakra set so that each crystal was on the appropriate chakra and added two aqua aura crystal clusters, one at each side of her neck. I then activated all the crystals with my quartz master crystal, and left her to simmer for 20 minutes. I prescribed the crystal chakra set, along with the aqua aura crystal cluster, which she needed to keep near her as much as possible and to hold for a minimum of 20–30 minutes every day. She was to follow her program for two weeks and then report back.

After two weeks she said that for the first four or five days she just couldn't put the aqua aura crystal down. She felt much better physically, and the neck brace was finally taken off. Over the rest of the period, she noticed she felt less anxious and had been expressing her feelings. It really surprised her when she found herself shouting at a colleague who had been upsetting her for years, and saying exactly what she thought of her!

Although whiplash was the condition Rosalie saw as the problem, the treatment was for the realignment and balance of the throat chakra, which had a subtle but profound effect on her overall healing.

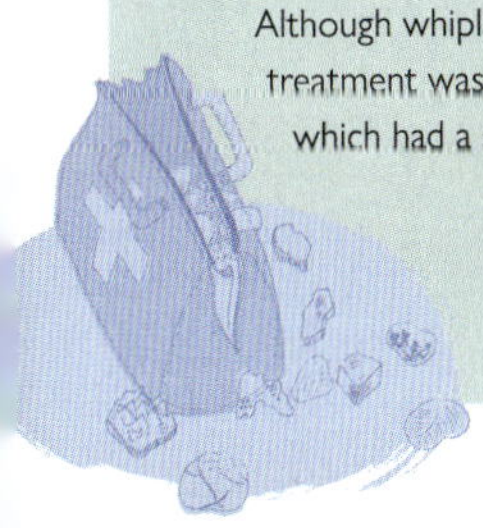

HEALING THE BROW CHAKRA

The sixth chakra is the brow chakra, also known as the third eye, which is located in the middle of the forehead above the eyebrows. It is the center of intuition, intellect, personal magnetism, and light. This is where creativity and inspiration combine, and psychic abilities and gifts are also focused here. When it is healthy and balanced, the sixth chakra helps to remove negative and selfish attitudes and facilitates intuition and wisdom.

LOCATION: Center of forehead, above eyebrows

CRYSTAL: Lapis lazuli

COLOR: Indigo

FRAGRANCE ASSOCIATION: Sandalwood

KEYWORDS: Mind, ideas, thoughts, dreams, psychic abilities, honesty, truth, intellectual abilities, feelings of adequacy, openness to new ideas and ideals, teaching

EMOTIONAL/MENTAL HEALING: When the brow chakra is dysfunctional, the mind can become unbalanced, negative ideas set in, and thoughts tumble aimlessly through our mind. This clogs up the creative paths, forming a fog in our mind that is difficult to see through. Our awareness drops and we lose touch with our senses. Intellectual and psychic abilities suffer, and we can feel blocked to new ideas and stuck in an emotional and mental rut. In extreme cases, mental illness can set in.

PHYSICAL HEALING: An imbalance in the brow chakra can result in headaches and migraines, learning difficulties and seizures, autism and Asperger's syndrome, neurological disorders, mental illness such as neuroses and personality disorders, also spinal conditions, sciatica and problems with nerve endings and synapses, sinusitis and all mucous problems, disorders of the eyes and ears, and problems with scalp and hair.

SPIRITUAL HEALING: The brow chakra is linked to our psychic and spiritual skills. We can all access these, as they are natural abilities everyone has. They work to enhance our physical senses, and denying them stunts our ability to experience in full the world around us. The brow chakra acts as a receiver for a whole host of information flowing into our energy system every second of the day. Most of the time this stream of data is processed subconsciously, rather like a program running in the background of a computer. As in a computer, in which we can bring a window to the front or open a new window, the brow chakra can be brought forward to bring extrasensory information into our conscious mind. This promotes clarity, inspiration, and innovation.

LIFESTYLE: A balanced brow chakra allows us to absorb and process information on many levels. It promotes the ability to learn from experience and pass this teaching on to others. This is the center of our nighttime dreams and also the dreams, goals, and ideals we have in life. It opens the door to possibilities.

ALTERNATIVE CRYSTALS: Sodalite, sapphire, moldavite, prehnite, cavansite, celestite, dumortierite, pietersite, tanzanite, fire agate, apophyllite, rutile

HEALING BENEFITS

The brow chakra is the thought center that clarifies and processes your everyday experiences—where your mind connects to the outside world and to your inner energy system.

This chakra maintains your mental health. By integrating your experiences, it keeps you sane when everything around you seems chaotic.

The brow chakra is the vital center of creative thought. It is where our inspiration, ideas, dreams, and goals begin; where eureka moments happen when the mind is still and quiet.

Mental stillness can be promoted by meditation; many traditional schools of meditation focus on the brow chakra to bring peace and tranquility to a troubled mind. By stilling the mind through crystal meditation (see page 42)

The brow chakra is linked to intuition, wisdom, and psychic abilities.

you can release worry and ease stress, freeing tension within the body. This promotes a quiet confidence, lifting depression and feelings of negativity and encouraging both mental and physical action.

Through the brow, or third eye, your psychic gifts act, enhancing your appreciation of the world around you. It connects your link to spirit (drawn down through your crown chakra via the brow to the throat), allowing you to express yourself truthfully. This simple ability releases stress and pent-up emotion, bringing order and clarity to your thoughts.

How to Tell If Your Brow Chakra Is Out of Balance

If the brow chakra is blocked, energy moves very slowly or doesn't flow at all, leading to imbalance in the mind and a fog of confusion. Also, events stemming from the loss of a dream or goal can often lead to detachment, causing an imbalance in this energy hot spot. An imbalance of the brow chakra can lead to symptoms such as the following:

- Mental illness
- Headaches and migraines
- Personality disorders
- Sinusitis
- Eye conditions
- Learning disabilities
- Feelings of negativity
- Lack of ambition

CRYSTALS FOR THE BROW CHAKRA

You can work with crystals to balance and heal the brow chakra by placing the crystal directly on the energy center on your body (see page 53), by carrying it with you all the time or, if suitable, taping it to your body with surgical tape. You can also try meditating with your chosen crystal and putting it by your bed or under your pillow at night. For more information on these and other healing techniques, refer to Chapter 5.

Lapis lazuli

Dumortierite

Sodalite

Pietersite

Sapphire

Tanzanite

Moldavite

Fire agate

Prehnite

Apophyllite

Cavansite

Rutile

Celestite

LAPIS LAZULI

Massive rock, cubic, and dodecahedral crystals—specimens almost always include lazurite, calcite, and pyrite.

Common sources: Afghanistan, Chile

Astrological association: Sagittarius

Chakra: Brow

Healing qualities: A "feel better stone" boosting all psychic abilities, natural gifts and skills, and bringing relaxation within its protective cocoon, lapis lazuli aids creative expression and wisdom. It enhances and brings clarity to dreams, boosts mental endurance, and helps to relieve insomnia. It dispels disorganization, lifting the depression that this can cause. It also promotes balance between yin and yang energies, which improves relationships.

Physical benefits: Boosts immune system and vitality. Benefits bones and bone marrow, throat, thymus, thyroid gland, and eustachian tubes. Helps dizziness, vertigo, hearing loss, and backache; good for detoxing. Lapis lazuli crystals help prevent illness and aid the repair of muscles and bone fractures.

SODALITE

Blue or blue and white masses, nodules and, rarely, dodecahedral and hexagonal prismatic crystals. May also be gray, green, yellow, white, red, or colorless.

Common source: Brazil

Astrological association: Sagittarius

Chakra: Brow

Healing qualities: A calming crystal that also boosts self-esteem, perception, creative expression, and endurance while easing mental unrest, oversensitivity, fear, confusion, and feelings of inadequacy. It is good for insomnia, mental health, and healing, and helps autism. It helps you to communicate feelings and ideas and is constructive in group situations.

Physical benefits: Good for balance, the lymphatic system, and the metabolism. Helps to combat signs of aging and calcium deficiency. Also helps diabetes and high blood pressure and is good for the healthy development of infants.

SAPPHIRE

Gem variety of corundum found in any color except red (which is ruby). Colors include yellow (oriental topaz), green (oriental emerald), violet (oriental amethyst), black, purple, pink, and white.

Common sources: India, Madagascar, Sri Lanka, Thailand

Astrological associations: Virgo, Libra, Sagittarius

Chakra: Brow

Healing qualities: Promotes the fulfillment of ambitions, dreams, and goals. Helps emotional balance, control of desires, joy, fun, intuition, wisdom, spiritual connection, and contact with spirit guides. It helps you see the beauty in everything, relieving depression, narrow-mindedness, and unhappiness.

Physical benefits: Good for heart, hormones, stomach, and all glands. Helps glandular fever, backache, nausea, infection, boils. Helps reduce bleeding and signs of aging. Has astringent properties. Record-keeper sapphire crystals help access the Akashic records and enhance astral travel. Star sapphire (showing asterism) enhances all the healing qualities above.

MOLDAVITE

This is green tektite that was originally created from a meteorite hitting the earth's surface, melting, and fusing with the earth. This is the resulting reformed natural glass material: part earth, part space.

Common alternative name: Valtava

Common source: Czech Republic (only source)

Astrological association: Scorpio

Chakras: Brow, heart

Healing qualities: Promotes mental balance and opens the mind to new possibilities and experiences. Good for altered mind states, such as meditation, dreams, and hypnosis. Enhances clairsentience.

Physical benefits: General tonic for the body. Aids balance.

PREHNITE

Massive botryoidal and globular structures, layered "plates," tabular, and prismatic crystals. Green, yellow, white, and brown colors.

Common source: Australia

Astrological association: Libra

Chakras: Brow, heart

Healing qualities: Helps you find your own true spiritual path through life. Aids prophecy, divination, visualization, meditation, dreams, and dream recall. Allows you to let go of emotions and thoughts you no longer need, bringing a state of calmness that permits inspiration. Lets you find that things flow around you, removing any sense of frustration.

Physical benefits: Good for kidneys, bladder, and connective tissue. Helps anemia and gout.

CAVANSITE

Orthorhombic crystals, sometimes in "flower" formation.

Common source: India

Astrological association: Aquarius

Chakra: Brow

Healing qualities: Enhances psychic abilities and protects healers from picking up empathetic pains from clients and taking home their "stuff" at the end of the day. It is a "feel good stone" that promotes new ideas.

Physical benefits: Good for eyes, teeth, and blood. Helps osteoporosis.

CELESTITE

Tabular orthorhombic crystals, nodules, and masses, principally in pale blue shades, but also in white, yellow, orange, red, and red-brown.

Common alternative name: Celestine

Common source: Madagascar

Astrological association: Gemini

Chakra: Brow

Healing qualities: A crystal linked very strongly to angels, promoting love with respect, creative expression, relaxation, music, art, and meditation. Helps dreams, dream recall, and astral travel, and banishes nightmares. Because it relieves stress and worry, allowing for clear thinking, it is good for mental activities involving complex ideas. It enhances natural abilities and balances yin and yang energies.

Physical benefits: Helps in the treatment of eye conditions, hearing problems, and speech impediments; relieves discomfort and pain. Good for detoxing.

DUMORTIERITE

Blue and pinkish brown masses.

Common source: Madagascar

Astrological association: Leo

Chakra: Brow

Healing qualities: Produces quiet confidence and patience that diminish excitability and stubbornness. Helps you to speak your mind and understand the cause of disease.

Physical benefits: Boosts stamina and is good for healing damaged ligaments and tendons.

PIETERSITE

Variety of tiger's eye, from gold to brown and shades of blue-gray, often in same specimen.

Common sources: Namibia, South Africa

Astrological association: Leo

Chakra: Brow

Healing qualities: Helps you to see the beauty in everything and aids visualizing during guided meditations and creative visualization. It is grounding, banishes fear, and aids access to the Akashic records.

Physical benefits: Combats the tiring effects of computer screens. Good for digestion, pineal gland, pituitary gland, endocrine glands, growth, sex drive, metabolism, blood pressure, and temperature balance (for example, in cases of fever or hypothermia).

TANZANITE

Variety of zoisite forming masses and prismatic striated crystals. Colors include blue, yellow, shades of blue-gray, and purple.

Common source: Tanzania

Astrological associations: Sagittarius, Gemini, Libra

Chakras: Brow, throat, crown

Healing qualities: Good for communication, it enhances all psychic abilities, contacting spirit guides, meditation, visualization, and magic.

Physical benefits: Good for skin and eyes. Helps exhaustion.

FIRE AGATE

Agate occurring as pebbles in brownish colors with flashes of "fire" owing to thin layers of limonite.

Common source: Mexico

Astrological association: Aries

Chakra: Brow

Healing qualities: Aids connection to spirit and gives a sense of spirituality. Enhances clairvoyance and acts as a psychic shield, giving protection and emotional control to conquer fear. It's an inspiring crystal that pushes you into action—doing and completing things.

Physical benefits: Good for everything to do with eyes such as sight, night vision, and treating eye disorders.

APOPHYLLITE

Cubic and pyramidal crystals, druses, and masses.
Commonly white or colorless, with a rarer green variety.

Common source: India

Astrological associations: Libra, Gemini

Chakras: Brow, crown

Healing qualities: Boosts brain power and mental activity. Promotes connection to spirit-enhancing psychic abilities such as scrying and clairvoyance, helping you see the truth, and also aids astral travel. A reflective crystal that helps to continue the meditative state after the meditation is finished.

Physical benefits: Good for eyesight, and the natural crystal pyramids can aid body rejuvenation.

RUTILE

Needlelike crystals, often penetrating quartz, rutilated quartz (see page 166), and prismatic crystals. Colors include silver, red, brown, black, yellow, and violet.

Common alternative name: Angel hair

Common source: Brazil

Astrological associations: Gemini, Taurus

Chakra: Brow

Healing qualities: Boosts the aura, creating a protective shield, and enhances astral travel and remote viewing. Helps you see the cause of dis-ease often seated within the aura. Brings mental balance and an acceptance of one's sexuality.

Physical benefits: Helps bronchitis, tired eyes, milk production in nursing mothers, veins, and wounds when it is applied as a topical elixir.

Crystal Clinic

John was a professional driver who suffered from severe migraines, resulting in blurred vision and temporary hearing loss, which could threaten his career. He wasn't very communicative—other than to say that he didn't think that crystal healing treatments would work, and to ask whether he had to believe in them. I'm often asked this question, to which the answer is no, you don't have to "believe"—just as you don't have to believe that bread will toast when you put it in the toaster and switch it on.

The first thing was to deal with the migraine symptoms, as this is so easy to do. Holding a dark amethyst crystal to the site of pain and doing all the things he would normally do during a migraine attack, such as lying down quietly in a darkened room, John soon discovered that the intense pain went away in about the same time that it took a well-known pharmaceutical migraine relief product to work. I explained that the more often he did this with the same dark amethyst crystal, the quicker it would work, and if he carried it with him all the time, then the frequency of attacks would reduce. He found this to be true for him.

The first treatment focused on the brow chakra, with lapis lazuli placed on the brow surrounded by four small crystals; apophyllite, cavansite, celestite, and fire agate. Amethyst was placed on the crown and blue lace agate on the throat chakra, and I energized each crystal with my quartz master crystal. I gave him a lapis lazuli crystal as well as the amethyst to work with during the week. The second treatment was similar but I placed fire agate on his eyelids instead of the four crystals around the brow chakra. The third treatment included the full crystal chakra set with quartz star on the brow. He reported feeling nothing in particular either during or after any of these treatments.

Before he arrived for the next treatment, I was considering recommending that John should try a different therapy that might be better for him. However,

recalling his skeptical approach, I thought we should keep going as I was certain that in his case changes were happening slowly. I repeated the previous treatment but changed the brow crystal to sapphire, hoping that it would open his mind to possibilities. He again said that he didn't feel anything, and he decided not to book another treatment.

About a month later he telephoned and booked a treatment. When he arrived, it was as if he was a different person. He had a new bounce in his step and a smile on his face. He told me that he had been an artist, designing posters and artwork for many theatrical shows, but had been severely criticized for a flop because "everyone" felt his publicity designs were awful on this particular show. He couldn't get any more work in the industry so had become a taxi driver. That's when his migraines had started.

Since he had come for the first treatment, both the severity and frequency of the attacks had greatly reduced. In the last four weeks he had started painting again and had designed magazine ads for a friend. Although he was still driving taxis, he remembered he was only doing this to make ends meet and had found a new and original surge of creativity. His eyesight and hearing were normal again.

John loved the idea of working with crystals himself and went on to train with me as a crystal healer and then a teacher. He still doesn't "believe" crystals work—but he has no need to because he "knows" they do.

HEALING THE CROWN CHAKRA

Located at the top of the head, the seventh chakra, or crown chakra, is the center of spirituality, enlightenment, and dynamic thought. It facilitates the flow of wisdom to you from the universe and connects you to the cosmic consciousness of all that is. All that can be known is already out there—we just need to tap into it. When it's healthy and balanced, this source of knowing helps you to distinguish between truth and illusion, and between ideals and self-defeating materialistic pursuits. It helps you see how to balance spirituality in the physical world. Self-limiting concepts, pride, and vanity are eliminated. It allows you to detach yourself from your emotions and experience genuine self-awareness.

LOCATION: Top of the head

CRYSTAL: Amethyst

COLOR: Violet

FRAGRANCE ASSOCIATION: Frankincense

KEYWORDS: Spirituality, connection to the universe and God, awareness, trust in life, seeing the bigger picture, values, ethics, courage, selflessness, inspiration, devotion, optimism, enthusiasm, originality, invention, perfection, fulfillment, completion, connection to angels and your unique potential

EMOTIONAL/MENTAL HEALING: When the crown chakra is out of balance, we feel unconnected. It can seem as if we are lost, wandering through life without purpose or direction. It feels as if our body, mind, and spirit are discombobulated. This is emotionally and mentally disturbing and can lead to lethargy and extreme physical dysfunction such as ME (myalgic encephalitis). We lose sight of the bigger picture and find ourselves focusing on insignificant detail. We get bogged down, stuck. Any optimism or enthusiasm evaporates as this energy sinks down through the other six chakras, producing almost any symptoms in the body. Where there appears to be no cause for a physical disorder, no specific emotional upset, and no sign of previous injury, the dysfunction of the crown chakra is almost certainly the cause.

PHYSICAL HEALING: Working with crystals on the crown chakra can help to relieve energy disorders, depression, and extreme sensitivity to your environment. It will aid whole-body healing, help maintain health, benefiting the brain, spine, and nervous system in particular, and will provide pain relief. It helps to relieve

The crown chakra connects you to the universe and cosmic consciousness.

neurological and autoimmune disorders, skin conditions, dementia, Parkinson's disease, and multiple sclerosis.

SPIRITUAL HEALING: The crown chakra is your connection to all the energy in the universe. The universe in this sense is God, Goddess, or a combination of several deities, Universal Energy, the Tao, Krishna, Buddha, Christ, the Source, or whatever you choose to call it. The name doesn't matter, but the connection does. It is the source of everything in life, our inspiration to go further, our guide providing the route map of our life plan, and our light that shows us the way.

LIFESTYLE: A balanced crown chakra full of healthy flowing energy can help bring out your uniqueness, your originality. It's what makes you special and can help you advance in just about every sphere of life, from career to relationships, from leisure and sport to spiritual pursuits.

ALTERNATIVE CRYSTALS: Charoite, spirit quartz, sugilite, labradorite, white calcite, danburite, Herkimer diamond, howlite, magnesite, petalite, rutilated quartz, selenite

HEALING BENEFITS

With the crown chakra in balance, you feel you understand your life and environment. It gives you an optimistic outlook, promoting action via the flow of energy through the other six chakras.

Each balanced energy hot spot supports and nourishes the next with this flow of healthy energy. The energy flows both ways, from the base chakra up to the crown chakra and down again. Once all your energy centers are balanced, it is easier to maintain the energy equilibrium throughout your body in times of stress. You have less "down time" and more "up time," leading to a healthy and fulfilled life. Your ego diminishes, allowing you to find an understanding that you are unique and at the same time part of everything else, giving you a humanitarian vision of society.

In an ideal world, all your chakras would be balanced all the time, bringing physical, mental, emotional, and spiritual health. But life happens, and so your chakras go in and out of balance. Regularly working with crystal chakra healing can bring and maintain this healthy balanced state.

How to Tell If Your Crown Chakra Is Out of Balance

Imbalance in the crown chakra is often the result of extreme trauma on any level. Traumatic experiences tend to have opposite effects with different people. Some experience a sudden and great connection, whereas others lose any connection they ever had. If the crown chakra is blocked, energy moves very slowly or doesn't move at all, leading to feelings of disconnection, pessimism, and lethargy. Common symptoms include the following:

- ME (myalgic encephalitis)
- Depression
- Nervous system disorders
- Skin conditions
- Dementia
- Vanity

CRYSTALS FOR THE CROWN CHAKRA

You can work with crystals to balance and heal the crown chakra by placing the crystal directly on the energy center on your body (see page 53), by carrying it with you all the time or, if suitable, taping it to your body with surgical tape. You can also try meditating with your chosen crystal and putting it by your bed or under your pillow at night. For more information on these and other healing techniques, refer to Chapter 5.

Amethyst

Herkimer diamond

Charoite

Howlite

Spirit quartz

Magnesite

Sugilite

Petalite

Labradorite

White calcite

Rutilated quartz

Danburite

Selenite

AMETHYST

Variety of quartz found as crystals or masses. Its classic purple color is the result of manganese and iron inclusions. Some rare varieties are almost black. Other varieties are chevron amethyst, with purple and white bands, and prasiolite, a green amethyst colored by mineral inclusions.

Common sources: Worldwide, especially Brazil, India, Madagascar, South Africa, Uruguay

Astrological associations: Pisces, Virgo, Aquarius, Capricorn

Chakra: Crown

Healing qualities: Calming and purifying, it improves temperament and alleviates addictions such as alcoholism and drunkenness, and addictive behavior such as OCD (obsessive-compulsive disorder). It reduces anger, combats violent tendencies, and calms passion, promoting chastity. It boosts the aura, giving protection, and promotes self-esteem and skills in decision-making, public speaking, and negotiation. This helps you to cope with responsibility, dispelling nervousness, tension, and oversensitivity. It supports emotional energy and aids emotional and mental balance, easing insomnia, while feelings such as grief and homesickness can also be relieved. Amethyst connects to Reiki and helps spirituality, spirit contact, purification for ceremonies, and meditation. It promotes flow and moving forward in life, making changes, business success, and the acquisition of wealth. It also magnifies the energy of other crystals and heals the cause of dis-ease.

Physical benefits: Good for the circulation, heart, and immune system, treating blood clots, and fighting bacterial and viral infections and cancer. It's also good for the stomach, liver, hormones, pineal, pituitary, and endocrine glands, skin, bones, and teeth, hearing and balance, posture, and sympathetic nervous system (the fight or flight response). Aids detoxing, improves posture, and helps headaches and migraines, acne, asthma, and ME (myalgic encephalitis). Drinking an amethyst elixir can help arthritis.

CHAROITE

Violet masses, sometimes with inclusions of white quartz and black manganese.

Common source: Russia

Astrological associations: Sagittarius, Scorpio

Chakra: Crown

Healing qualities: Brings your spiritual experiences into your physical world and breaks cycles, releasing old relationships. It aids the mind by supporting analysis and attention span, and can help autism and ADHD. It promotes being in the moment and seeing opportunities, meditation, clairvoyance, intuition, and moving forward in life.

Physical benefits: Good for eyes, heart, and pulse rate; useful for detoxing (as an elixir); helps headaches, general aches and pains, and pancreatic and liver damage, such as sclerosis of the liver.

SPIRIT QUARTZ

Amethyst (purple) or quartz (white), sometimes with brownish orange iron inclusions or surface staining.

Common source: South Africa

Astrological associations: Pisces, Virgo, Aquarius, Capricorn

Chakra: Crown

Healing qualities: Enhances meditation, giving insight into your inner self and your dark side, bestowing a sense of belonging, and dispelling loneliness and grief. It boosts self-esteem and patience, allowing you to release and revitalize emotions by removing fear of success and helping you deal with obsessive behavior. It bonds groups in work environments and sports, promoting team-building. It increases fertility and abundance and helps things flow well in life. Aids astral travel, dreams, past experiences, past lives, rebirthing, and extra-sensory perception, and it provides protection.

Physical benefits: Good for detoxing and, if drunk as an elixir, can relieve skin allergies.

SUGILITE

Masses and rare tiny crystals.

Common alternative names: Lavulite, royal lavulite, royal azel

Common source: South Africa

Astrological association: Virgo

Chakra: Crown

Healing qualities: Helps you to understand the mind–body link in disease. Aids mental balance, promoting confidence, courage, creativity, and forgiveness and releasing hostility, anger, jealousy, prejudice, and despair. Inspires spiritual love, spirit contact, and an understanding of your life

path. Good for eccentricity; it doesn't "cure" it, but helps you be who you are. It is beneficial for Indigo Children (children who possess paranormal abilities) and also for children with learning difficulties.

Physical benefits: Because of the mind–body link, it is helpful in the treatment of most illnesses and physical discomfort, and in whole body healing. Also helps dyslexia, headaches, and epilepsy. Good for adrenal, pineal, and pituitary glands.

LABRADORITE

Masses of plagioclase feldspar with albite, occasionally forming tabular crystals, gray-green, pale green, blue, colorless or gray-white in color. The brilliant flashes of blue, red, gold, and green are the result of light interference within the structure of the minerals' composition.

Common alternative names: Black moonstone, Labrador moonstone, Labrador feldspar, spectrolite

Common sources: Canada, Madagascar, Norway

Astrological associations: Sagittarius, Scorpio, Leo

Chakra: Crown

Healing qualities: Allows magic to happen and promotes linkage between the right and left hemispheres of the brain, increasing interaction between them. This is the mental connection between magic and science, between intuition and intellect. It stabilizes the aura and enhances the flow of energy between the aura and the chakras. Promotes mental sharpness, inspiration, and originality, allowing you to see many possibilities at once and reducing insecurity, anxiety, and stress.

Physical benefits: Good for digestion and eyes. Helps the treatment of warts.

WHITE CALCITE

"Dogtooth" crystals.

Common source: Brazil

Astrological association: Cancer

Chakra: Crown

Healing qualities: Clears the mind, helping to see through the fog of confusion. Also helps to find answers in meditation.

Physical benefits: Good for kidneys, liver, and lymphatic system. Aids detoxing.

DANBURITE

Clear, white, pink, yellow, and lilac prismatic striated crystals.

Common sources: Mexico, USA

Astrological association: Leo

Chakra: Crown

Healing qualities: Facilitates getting back into the world after an absence for any reason, such as breakdown, drug dependency, or hospitalization. Encourages socialization and alleviates postoperative depression.

Physical benefits: Relieves muscle stiffness. Good for gallbladder and liver. Aids detoxing and weight gain.

HERKIMER DIAMOND

Clear, stubby, double-terminated quartz crystal.

Common source: Herkimer County, New York, USA (only source—other "diamond-style" quartz crystals are available from Pakistan, Mexico, and Romania; these are not the same and, although they may be wonderful crystals in themselves, are not covered here)

Astrological association: Sagittarius

Chakra: Crown

Healing qualities: Promotes spontaneity, being in the moment, relaxation, and new beginnings; alleviates stress, tension, and fear. Helps to focus attunement processes, whether to energies, people, places, deities, ceremony, Reiki, or anything else. Aids memory and psychic abilities.

Physical benefits: Good for metabolism and DNA and RNA replication. Helps recovery from most injuries, toxins, and radiation, and supports detoxing.

HOWLITE

White or off-white nodules, masses, and, rarely, crystals. Often dyed to imitate more expensive stones.

Common source: USA

Astrological association: Gemini

Chakra: Crown

Healing qualities: Aids emotional expression and calm communication, helps discernment, and reduces stress, selfishness, anger, boisterousness, and vulgarity. Promotes action and the achievement of goals. Good for memory and study.

Physical benefits: Boosts immune system, good for teeth and bones, and relieves pain.

MAGNESITE

Masses and nodules that look a bit like 200-million-year-old chewing gum! Usually white, but also gray, brown, and yellow. Also forms rhombohedral, prismatic, tabular, and scalenohedral crystals, but these are rare.

Common sources: Worldwide, especially South Africa

Astrological association: Aries

Chakra: Crown

Healing qualities: Aids meditation and visualization; grounds intellect; promotes passion and love.

Physical benefits: Helps injured tendons and ligaments, convulsions, PMS (premenstrual syndrome), and body odor. Good for cardiac arteries and eases associated disorders, such as effects of high cholesterol levels, arteriosclerosis, and angina. Also good for bones and teeth. Balances body temperature and therefore helps fever, chill, and hypothermia. Supports cellular detoxing.

PETALITE

Clear, white, pink, gray, green, white, and red and white masses

Common sources: Brazil, Madagascar

Astrological association: Leo

Chakra: Crown

Healing qualities: Promotes a spiritual connection to God, angels, spirit guides, and totem animals. Enhances shamanic vision quests and astral travel and helps you to stay grounded during meditation. It helps you have peace of mind and the courage of your convictions. Reduces clumsiness. Good for the aura, development of all psychic abilities, and yin and yang energy balance.

Physical benefits: Helps ME (myalgic encephalitis), cancer, and tumors. Good for eyelids, eyebrows, and muscle and joint flexibility. Supports detoxing.

RUTILATED QUARTZ

Quartz with silver or golden threads of rutile.

Common alternative name: Angel hair

Common source: Brazil

Astrological associations: All star signs

Chakras: Crown, brow

Healing qualities: Brings calmness and balance, which helps mental health and healing, deep depression, despair, breakdown, emotional blockages, and negativity.

Physical benefits: Promotes vitality and strength, boosts the immune system, activates nerves, helps neuralgia and Parkinson's disease, and is good for tissue regeneration, weight gain, reducing signs of aging, and helping to maintain a youthful appearance.

SELENITE

Crystallized form of gypsum, clear or white.

Common sources: Canada, Mexico, Morocco

Astrological associations: Taurus. Also linked with the moon (named after Selene, the Greek goddess of the moon)

Chakra: Crown

Healing qualities: Good for emotions linked to cycles and repeated patterns, whether physical, such as the menstrual cycle, or behavioral.

Physical benefits: Helps the effects of leakage from mercury amalgam fillings, light sensitivity, and conditions associated with free radicals, including tumors, and age spots. Helps skin conditions such as acne, eczema, and psoriasis, and is good for skin elasticity, wrinkle prevention, and hair loss, encouraging a youthful appearance. Also good for the spine and menstrual cycle. It boosts fertility and sex drive. Helps epilepsy and promotes longevity.

Crystal Clinic

Tracy was only 18 years old but showed symptoms of depression, apathy, and lethargy. She spent little time with her friends and had no interests or boyfriends. Her parents were distraught. She was very intelligent but couldn't see the point of going to university.

I started the first treatment with a crystal chakra set, adding quartz stars to all the chakras after checking their direction with my pendulum. Working with the quartz master crystal, I realized that the crown and sacral chakras needed more work. These areas felt sticky, as if trying to push my crystal through treacle. Tracy said she felt uncomfortable when I was working over these two areas. I gave her carnelian and amethyst to work with, asking her to keep them with her and play with either or both however and as often as she liked.

At the start of the next treatment, she said that she had played with her crystals a lot and had felt much better by the middle of the week, but that it had worn off and she was back to how she had been. First I held the pendulum over each of these two chakras, asking, "Is this chakra the key to unlocking Tracy's problem?" Over the sacral chakra I received a negative response and over the crown chakra a positive one. I then repeated the treatment from the previous week. This time the sacral chakra felt clearer but the crown was still sticky. I reworked the crown area with my quartz master crystal, moving it counterclockwise. Tracy became emotional. I gave her two spirit quartz crystals to help release trapped emotion, then resumed the treatment. She started crying, but as I continued she gradually relaxed.

After the treatment she said that although the session had been tough, she now felt wonderful. She asked to take the quartzes, promising to return them.

Tracy didn't turn up for her next appointment. About five years later she walked into my shop and told me that the spirit quartz had changed her life. She went to university, married the boyfriend she met there, and now had a successful career. She then produced two spirit quartz crystals, duly returning them as promised.

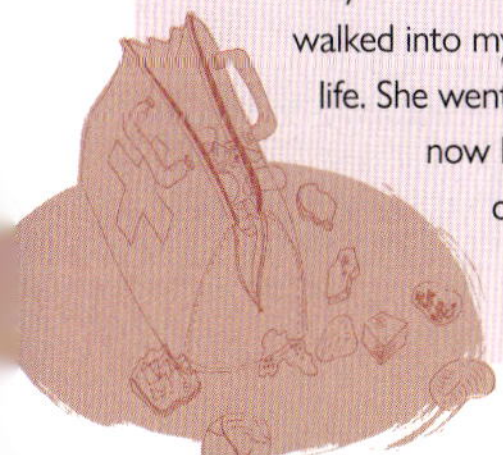

CRYSTALS FOR ALL THE CHAKRAS

This section deals with crystals that will work on any and all chakras. Each has its own unique properties that may be helpful in the treatment of specific conditions.

TOURMALINE

Vertically striated prismatic crystals in most colors: green verdelite, blue indicolite, pink elbaite, red rubellite, yellow tsilasite, black schorl, brown dravite, watermelon (green or blue with pink center, or colors reversed), bicolors, tricolors, lime green often with white center, colorless achroite, and lavender.

Common sources: Brazil, Pakistan

Astrological association: Libra

Chakras: All

Healing qualities: Gives protection on all levels, from simple accidents to psychic attack and evil curses! It brings balance in all situations, is calming, and promotes creativity, inspiration, self-confidence, new challenges, negotiation skills, awareness, psychic abilities, healing ability, and connection to your inner self, people, your environment, and spirit. It is good for mental health and healing and helps breakdown, blockages, restless mind, schizophrenia, contrariness, victim mentality, a troubled mind, negativity, fear, and worrying too much about what others think. Helps balance left and right brain hemispheres and yin and yang energies, and boosts the aura. Aids group work and laughter therapy.
Physical benefits: Good for digestion, lymphatic system, and bladder. Supports detoxing and helps low blood pressure. Tourmaline wand crystals (long, thin crystals) focus energy to areas where it is most needed, support affirmations, and are excellent for aura healing.

QUARTZ CRYSTAL

Clear or white hexagonal crystals and masses, sometimes with inclusions.
Common alternative names: Clear quartz, rock crystal
Common sources: Worldwide, especially USA (Arkansas), Brazil, China, Madagascar, Russia, South Africa
Astrological associations: All star signs
Chakras: All
Healing qualities: Channels any energy so will help with any condition, whether physical, emotional, mental, or spiritual. Also quartz specifically helps with meditation and focusing the mind. It is a "feel better stone," improving your quality of life, making you feel happier, dispelling negativity, and reenergizing your zest for life in all situations.

Physical benefits: Helps all conditions and, specifically, any pain or discomfort, general malaise, low energy, ME (myalgic encephalitis), ear problems such as infections or tinnitus, diabetes, and multiple sclerosis. Good for balance, the heart, the spine, and weight loss.

TITANIUM QUARTZ

Quartz crystal bonded with titanium and niobium.

Common alternative names: Flame aura quartz, rainbow quartz, rainbow aura quartz, aura quartz, royal aura

Common source: USA

Astrological associations: All star signs

Chakras: All

Healing qualities: A "feel better crystal" that centers emotions. It helps you see another's point of view and stimulates energy flow and change. Good for meditation, it helps you find your own true path through life and is helpful for career decisions. It also improves your ability to see auras.

Physical benefits: Good for anything to do with body fluids, such as helping dehydration and water retention. Helps prevent illness, quells fever, and helps bone cancer, and multiple sclerosis.

DIAMOND

Octahedral, dodecahedral, and trapezohedral crystals. Colors include clear, white, yellow, blue, brown, pink, red, orange, and green.

Common sources: Central and southern Africa, Australia, Brazil, India, Russia, Venezuela

Astrological associations: Aries, Leo, Taurus

Chakras: All

Healing qualities: Gives protection by emanating positive energy in any situation, repelling negativity. Acts as a spiritual detox, promoting spiritual awareness and right and left brain interaction. This clears the "fog" in the mind, helping with a myriad of issues and emotions such as love, liking yourself, relationships, purity, cowardice, anger, and childhood issues. Diamond enhances creativity, imagination, ingenuity, invention, change, and new beginnings, helping you to start new projects that will lead to abundance. It boosts the aura and increases the effects of all other crystals.

Physical benefits: Good for metabolism and eyesight, and aids detoxing.

ANGEL AURA QUARTZ

Quartz crystal bonded with platinum and silver.

Common alternative name: Opal aura

Common source: USA

Astrological associations: All star signs

Chakras: All

Healing qualities: Helps you to connect to angels and the angelic realms. Boosts the aura, creating a protective field around you. Aids karma, supports empathy, love, peace, and harmony, and keeps you well. It is recommended for people working in the caring professions. Good for accessing the Akashic records.

Physical benefits: Helps headaches, backache, and tired blurred vision.

PYRITE

Cubic and dodecahedral crystals, occasionally flattened (pyrite suns) and masses. It becomes more golden with oxidation and may replace many minerals, so it can be found in many other formations and in combination with other minerals.

Common alternative names: Iron pyrites, fool's gold

Common sources: Peru, Spain, UK, USA

Astrological association: Leo

Chakras: All

Healing qualities: Helps thought processes, promotes leadership qualities, and gives protection, especially against negativity, accidents, and disruption from noisy neighbors.

Physical benefits: Gives an instant energy boost. Good for the circulation, cell regeneration, digestion, brain and memory, bones, and lungs. Helps bronchitis, infection, inflammation, fever, varicose veins, conditions caused by pollutants, and radiation sickness. It also helps prevent snoring.

TOURMALINATED QUARTZ

Quartz with black tourmaline crystal rods growing through it.

Common alternative name: Tourmaline in quartz

Common source: Brazil

Astrological associations: All star signs

Chakras: All

Healing qualities: Dispels negative childhood experiences and related behavior patterns, depression, fear, and nervous exhaustion. Aids problem-solving.
Physical benefits: Good for nervous system.

TIBETAN QUARTZ

Clear quartz crystals, often with black hematite inclusions.
Common source: Tibet (China)—only source, note that a lot of Chinese Himalayan quartz is sold as Tibetan
Astrological associations: All star signs
Chakras: All
Healing qualities: A "feel good stone" that promotes a spiritual connection and helps you be more direct.
Physical benefits: See quartz crystal (page 169).

DIOPTASE

Brilliant small emerald green prismatic crystals and masses.
Common sources: Democratic Republic of Congo, Namibia, Russia, USA
Astrological associations: Sagittarius, Scorpio
Chakras: All
Healing qualities: Aids emotional and mental balance; relieves the feeling of being oppressed and paranoia. Clears stuck emotions so you can live in the moment. Helps you understand the cause of dis-ease. Promotes change, renewal of goals and ideals, and past-life experiences. Helps yin and yang energy balance and attracts abundance.

Physical benefits: Boosts vitality and the immune response; encourages nutritional balance. Good for the circulation, heart, and lungs, and helps blood pressure, angina, and varicose veins. It's also beneficial to the stomach and digestion, helping IBS (irritable bowel syndrome), ulcers, nausea, and diarrhea. It promotes the healthy development of babies, helps dizziness and Ménière's disease. Taken as an elixir, it can relieve pain, especially headaches, migraines, and postoperative discomfort.

SPHENE

Masses, layered "plates," and flattened wedge-shaped crystals, in many colors.

Common alternative name: Titanite

Common sources: Canada, Mexico, Pakistan, Russia, USA

Astrological association: Sagittarius

Chakras: All

Healing qualities: Good for the study of astronomy and astrology. It is physically calming during shock and situations of extreme stress.

Physical benefits: It is good for teeth, helps muscle sprains and strains, reduces fever, relieves sunburn, and boosts the immune system and red blood cell production.

CHAPTER 5

HEALING TECHNIQUES

This chapter presents the complete crystal chakra healing system in practice. Here, discover all the ways of working with this system of healing, from preparation to giving a full treatment and closing the session. There are also sections on self-healing, including aura cleansing, and distant healing, so you can learn to work with crystals to heal remotely.

A HEALING SPACE

Before you begin any treatments, you need a special space to work in. In an ideal world, this would be a room set aside for the purpose—in your home, at work, in a clinic, or in a healing/therapy center. Even if it's not possible to have a separate room, there are still many things you can do to create a temporary healing space.

Whether it is to be permanent or temporary, this must be a safe space both in practical terms and in how the room feels. It needs to be clean and energetically cleansed, so having a ritual to cleanse and dedicate the room each time you use it is helpful. This can be drawn from your belief system or you can use a traditional procedure for cleansing.

HARNESSING THE ENERGIES OF THE ELEMENTS

Traditional cleansing can be done using the technique of smudging, which uses four items linked to the four elements—Earth, Air, Fire, and Water. This brings the particular energies of each element into your healing space, to enhance the special atmosphere you are creating.

The herbs in a smudge stick (a bundle of dried herbs such as sage) represent *Earth* element. Light one end of the smudge stick, blow out the flame, and it will smolder in a similar way to an incense stick. Now use a large feather, representing the element of *Air*, to direct the smoke, signifying *Fire*, around the room.

Place crystals in your healing space to create a calming atmosphere.

Pay special attention to all the corners of the healing room, where energy has a habit of stagnating. While you are wafting the smoke with the feather, hold a large seashell under the smudge stick, which will connect you to the *Water* element, as well as catching any falling embers to avoid damage to the floor covering.

CREATING A SENSE OF COMFORT AND ATMOSPHERE

Your healing work space must also be comfortable, with cushions or a therapy bed. You could even cover a sturdy dining table with blankets and cushions if this is the only suitable surface available to you. You need to remember that you are creating a relaxed space for your clients and for you to work in.

The room should be comfortably warm —resembling neither a sauna nor a refrigerator—and ventilated with fresh air if at all possible. Burn some incense or fragranced oils if the room is well ventilated (but do not use pure essential oils unless you are aware of their possible contraindications). Play some relaxing music quietly in the background.

Where possible, design the lighting so it can be dimmed to give a warm glow. Many therapists like to introduce candles (but be aware of the fire risk) as the flame "brings in the light," emphasizing that you are working for the highest good.

Make sure your crystals are cleansed (see pages 27–30), and then arrange them in the room so they can be selected quickly and easily. If this doesn't offer a pleasing view of them for your clients, then consider arranging a separate crystal display to dazzle them when they first arrive. Add flowers, plants, or other sources of color, such as scarves or cards. If you wish, you could represent the seven chakra colors.

Candles create ambience in your sacred space.

BEGINNING TREATMENT

When you have prepared your healing area (see pages 176–178), sit quietly in it for a few minutes and meditate or focus on what you are about to do. Center yourself and feel a connection to the ground, your crystals, and the room.

If you feel unconnected or ungrounded, try holding one or two hematite stones in your hands for a couple of minutes. This is a quick yet effective method of grounding. Keeping hematite in your pocket, wearing it, or having a larger display piece in your healing space will help if you sense you are becoming ungrounded while giving a treatment. Placing two pieces of hematite at your clients' feet at the start of the treatment is also one way of insuring they feel grounded afterward.

GROUNDING VISUALIZATION

This visualization exercise is another effective way of grounding yourself. Imagine you are standing barefoot on a muddy riverbank. In your mind, feel your feet sinking into the mud, which is oozing around your feet and squelching between your toes. Hold this image and sensation for a few minutes, allowing yourself to feel that you are sinking deeper and deeper into the mud.

Hematite has a grounding effect.

DIAGNOSIS AND DISCOVERY

Whether you are working with crystals to heal clients, family, or friends, begin with the procedure explained in the Practical Exercise shown opposite to discover where you need to focus your efforts. (If you wish, you can also use the technique when self-healing—see pages 194–195.)

PLACING THE CHAKRA CRYSTALS

When you have decided what chakra crystals to work with and where to place them, and your client is still lying down and deeply relaxed, you can place the appropriate crystal on each chakra. Be direct and firm but gentle—being tentative or indecisive is very irritating for the client. If the crystal doesn't end up exactly where you wanted it on the chakra, or if it slips or even falls off the body, just leave it. As long as it is close to the area you aimed for, it will be doing some good; and the more you practice, the more decisive you will become.

TIP

If you find that you are picking up empathic emotions or physical pain from your clients, wear a tourmaline pendant to protect you while giving treatments.

PRACTICAL EXERCISE: Diagnosing Problems

- With your client lying down, hold your pendulum 2–4 in/5–10 cm over their base chakra and ask the pendulum, "Is this chakra out of balance?" This wording means that the question essentially includes everything that could be wrong with the base chakra and the physical area (both internal and external) and emotions that it supports.
- If you get a "no" response—in other words, your pendulum is saying that the chakra is not out of balance—then place the appropriate standard chakra crystal on the base chakra.
- If the response is a "yes"—meaning that the chakra is out of balance—then use your pendulum to select a helpful crystal from all the possible crystals for the base chakra and from the crystals that work on any chakra.
- Working up the body from the base chakra, repeat this process for the six remaining chakras.

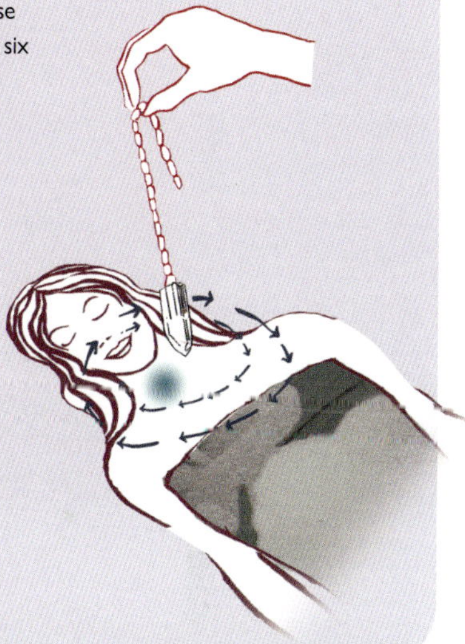

With quartz stars, all the crystals should point in the same direction relative to the chakra crystal, that is "in" (see left illustration) or "out" (see right illustration).

QUARTZ STARS

To enhance the flow of energy, you can surround a chakra crystal with four mini quartz crystal points. This is known as a quartz star.

Inward pointing: If the crystals are pointing inward, they will focus more energy into the chakra, enhancing the action of the chakra crystal. This arrangement is good for "blasting" through blocks of energy and for cleaning out old or stagnant energies that are no longer needed. A layout in which all seven quartz stars are pointing inward is also wonderful for reenergizing the body.

Outward pointing: If the crystals are pointing outward, away from the chakra crystal, they will help to gently release trapped energy from this area. This arrangement is calming and relaxing, and many people liken it to a soft massage.

Decisions through Dowsing

Your pendulum can be used in the following way to decide whether quartz stars are appropriate. After you have placed all seven chakra crystals on the body, dowse each chakra, asking the question, "Does this chakra need a quartz star?"

- If the answer is *no*, it means that no quartz star is needed on that chakra, so you can move on to the next chakra and repeat the above question.
- If the answer is *yes*, then ask, "Do the crystals need to point in?" If the answer to that question is yes, then place them with the points directed in. If the answer is no, then place them with the points directed outward, away from the chakra crystal.

Star Patterns

In any single treatment, all, some, or none of the seven chakras may need quartz stars. Here are some of the possible layouts of quartz stars:

- Stars all pointing the same way
- Stars all pointing the same way except for one star pointing the other way
- Stars alternately pointing in and out
- Stars pointing in or out at random

OTHER CRYSTALS

Now you are ready to check whether any other crystals are required. The easiest way to do this is simply to ask your pendulum, "Does my client need any other crystals?" Most of the time the answer will be no, but occasionally one or more crystals will be needed. When this is the case, you will need to dowse the selection of crystals you have available (because your previous question was really, "With the selection of crystals I have here right now, does my client need any other crystals?"). Once again, trust your intuition—if any crystal jumps out at you while you are dowsing, take it. You may also wish to look up your client's particular symptoms and select the recommended crystals.

The placement of any extra crystals is unlikely to tie in with the chakras, because the chakra crystals have already been selected and placed, and at any rate may not obviously link to the physical symptom you are treating. The additional crystal may be placed on a meridian or in the aura around the body, so that it is at the site of the energy block, even if that is quite far from the location of the actual symptom caused by the energy block.

You can dowse over a selection of crystals to discover if more are needed for a treatment.

PRACTICAL EXERCISE:
Placement through Gridding

The process by which you decide where to place any additional crystals is called gridding, because it involves, in effect, creating a grid over your client's body. The grid is traced with your pendulum in the following way.

- Hold one of the additional crystals in your non-dominant hand (for example, your left hand if you are right-handed) and your pendulum in the other. Ask your pendulum the question, "Should this crystal go here?" As you do so, pass your pendulum quite quickly over the center line that runs the length of your client's body, starting below the feet and finishing just above their head. You are looking for a positive response from your pendulum, so ignore any "no" answers. Just keep moving the pendulum until you get a distinct yes.
- Now move the pendulum laterally (from beyond one side of the client's body to just past the other side of their body), passing over your previously discovered positive point, until you have a positive answer. This is the point at which this additional crystal should be placed.
- Repeat steps 1 and 2 for any other additional crystals you have selected. The more you practice this, the easier and quicker the process will become.

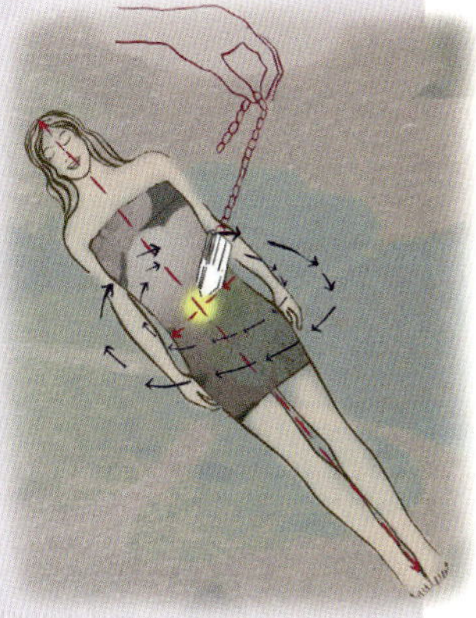

PRACTICAL EXERCISE:
Using Your Hand as a Pendulum

You can try using your hand in the same way as you would the pendulum. This will help you to sense the energy of your client's body and will link in with your internal pendulum (see pages 25–26) and ability to sense energies. Although the technique takes quite a lot of practice, it speeds up the selection and placement of additional crystals, and so is worth persevering with.

- First, try just sensing the energy of your client. (Let them know what you are going to do and ask for their permission.) Hold the flat palm of your hand 2–4 in/5–10 cm above your client's body and pass it over them as you would the pendulum, paying particular attention to the chakras. Look for any change of feeling in the palm of your hand. Over a chakra it may become warmer or cooler, or feel lighter or heavier, or you may be aware of the air above the chakra being dense or "sticky."
- At the same time, be conscious of your internal pendulum and its answers—you don't have to ask your internal pendulum any questions, as it is part of you and knows what you're thinking. Do this often enough and your internal pendulum will naturally cut in. Most people will eventually be able to site the additional crystals just by looking and trusting their internal pendulum, without going through the process of gridding.

AURA HEALING WITH CRYSTALS

Another way of working is in the auric field, a method that can be combined with any of the other crystal chakra healing techniques. The crystals are placed on the floor 6–20 in/15–50 cm around your client to encircle them (or you, if you are self-healing). From the aura crystals listed on page 64, you can select two types that you alternate around the circle, or just one type that you place all the way around, or one of each type.

Clockwise from top left: Amazonite, green moss agate, labradorite, and titanium quartz can all help heal the aura.

The effect of this treatment is to support and heal the aura. It can produce profound changes on many levels resulting in an air of confidence that touches others, reassuring and inspiring both you and them. It's also a useful technique for clients who, for some reason, cannot practice the laying on of stones system—for example, if they cannot lie down.

By placing one of each of the aura crystals around the outer edge of the room, you can use this approach to create a temporary healing space or to enhance your permanent healing room. The additional benefits are that both your client and you receive an aura treatment without effort.

ACTIVATING THE CRYSTALS

All the crystals you have placed on and around your client's body will begin working as soon as they are positioned, but you can help them to work even more by using the technique explained in the Practical Exercise on page 188. Activating crystals involves activating the crystals you are working with by means of your quartz master crystal. The healing effect upon the client can be profound.

PRACTICAL EXERCISE: Activating the Crystals

- With your dominant hand, hold your quartz master crystal 1–2 in/2.5–5 cm over the crystal that is highest on or above the body. This is usually the crown chakra crystal, but you may have placed another additional crystal above this.
- While pointing your quartz master crystal toward your target, move it slowly in a clockwise circle until you notice a change. Common indicators include:
  - A warm crystal becoming cool or a cool one changing to warm
  - Finding it difficult to move the crystal through the air at first, as if it's going through molasses, but becoming easier as the energy below it clears
  - Beginning to tingle, or stopping tingling
- Once you notice a change, whether it is one of the above indicators or some other change, move to the next crystal and repeat the previous steps. Do this for all the crystals on the body. If you find that you're not feeling a change at first, don't be concerned, as it sometimes takes a little practice. In this case just spend a minute or two on each crystal on the body with your quartz master crystal.
- For any quartz stars, hold your master crystal in your dominant hand 1–2 in/2.5–5 cm above them with its termination pointing toward these crystals. If the quartz star is pointing inward toward the chakra crystal, move the master crystal slowly in a clockwise direction. If the quartz star is directed away from the chakra crystal, move the master crystal counterclockwise.

ENDING THE SESSION

When you have completed all of the full treatment procedures, as well as removing the crystals from your client's body, you may need to comb and seal the aura, help your client to feel grounded, and cleanse your room and crystals.

REMOVING THE CRYSTALS

At the end of the treatment, remove all crystals on and around the body. Start at the crown and, irrespective of the order in which you placed the crystals, take them off one at a time, going down the body. As with placing crystals, don't fiddle with them or with your client's clothing or hair as you remove them. If a crystal has slipped during the treatment, you can retrieve it when your client gets up to leave.

COMBING AND SEALING THE AURA

Crystal chakra healing treatments move energy and release unneeded emotions and thoughts, some of which may still be in your client's aura. After a treatment, it is not uncommon for these old energies to linger.

Combing, or brushing down, the aura following a healing treatment settles any wayward energy and removes all emotions and thoughts that are no longer needed. Receiving this practice (see the Practical Exercise, page 191) feels pleasant and comforting, rather like a very gentle release of something you can't quite identify. Following treatment, many clients report that they can sense the crystal passing through their aura and that they feel lighter.

TIP

Have a soft receptacle such as a wicker basket or a tray covered with silk in which to collect your crystals. This will reduce any noise while you are gathering them up.

Sealing the aura (see Practical Exercise, page 192) cleanses it of unneeded energy remaining after the healing is complete. It also locks in the treatment, helping it to last much longer, which results in ongoing and deeper healing even after your client has left. Your intention is very important during this part of the process.

FINISHING

Check that your client is awake (they sometimes fall fast asleep!) and ask them to get up slowly. Sometimes it's nice for them to roll onto their side and lie in the fetal position for a few minutes first.

Some clients will want to talk to you about their experience and others won't. This is not a reflection on your ability or how you have conducted the session.

Brushing the aura after treatment helps settle the client and remove any turbulent residual energy.

GROUNDING

Your client may feel a bit spacey after a crystal chakra healing treatment. Ask yourself if they look and sound grounded, and don't let them get into their car and drive off if they're ungrounded.

To ground your client, either place two hematite stones by their feet at the start of the treatment, as mentioned on page 179, or give them two pieces to hold, one in each hand, at the end of the treatment.

You should have grounded yourself before you commenced the treatment (see page 179), but if you are feeling at all spacey afterward, hold two pieces of hematite, as above.

PRACTICAL EXERCISE: Combing the Aura

- After removing all the crystals, while your client is still lying down, comb through their aura, working with the side of your quartz master crystal as if it were a hairbrush. Start above the head and work down the body past the feet, holding your crystal 2–4 in/5–10 cm from the body. Treat the aura as if you were brushing long hair.
- If you find a knot, go over it gently several times until it feels free.
- You need to cover the whole body and both sides so you may have to repeat the steps above several times, depending on the girth of your client.
- When you are combing the aura with your quartz master crystal, it may feel sticky or the aura may feel thick and muggy as you pass your crystal through it. Treat these feelings in the same way as knots.

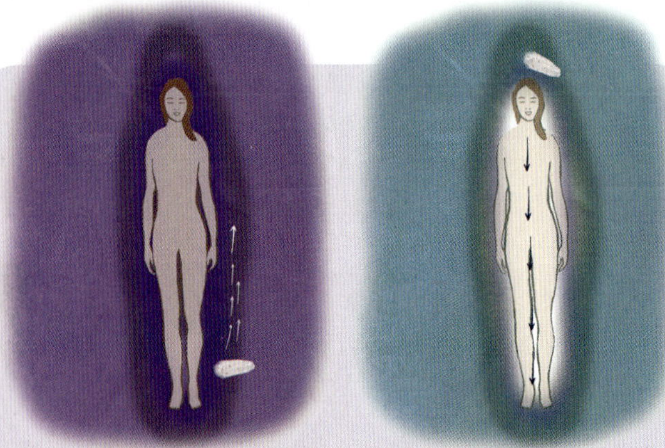

PRACTICAL EXERCISE: Sealing the Aura

- Stand or kneel next to your client close to their heart, on the same side as your dominant hand—if you're right-handed, you will be on the right side of their body. This makes it easier for you to reach over their whole body. Working with your quartz master crystal about 4 in/10 cm from your client's body, start at their head and move the side of the crystal through the aura to their feet, as if you were combing the aura (see page 191). Do this with the intent of the crystal picking up any unneeded energies still bubbling around in the aura.
- Lifting the crystal as high as you can, and pointing the termination out and up, move it back to the head in a high arc. Imagine that you and your quartz master crystal are pushing your client's aura out, expanding it as far as you can.
- Move the side of the crystal down the body to the feet, ending with it pointing away from the client and toward a window or door. Intend that anything not needed by your client flows with the cleansing crystal energy from your client out of the room.

CLEANSING

During the treatment, your client will have released unhelpful and unneeded energy. Some of this will have been absorbed by your crystals, with the rest being at large in the room. It is therefore important that you cleanse your crystals and the room before you see another client and place the same crystals on them, or close down and put your crystals away. Uncleansed crystals will hold your previous client's energy, which will be picked up by your next client.

An easy way to cleanse the room between clients is with Tibetan cymbals. The sound will raise the vibration, shaking any negative energy out. Pay particular attention to where your client was lying.

After you finish all your treatments for the day, follow the instructions on pages 27–30 to cleanse your crystals before you put them away, and then cleanse the room with a smudge stick (see pages 176–177). If you feel that your energy is sticky or you feel unclean, stand under a shower and let the water flow over your crown chakra and down your body. Pretend you are a crystal being cleansed under running water.

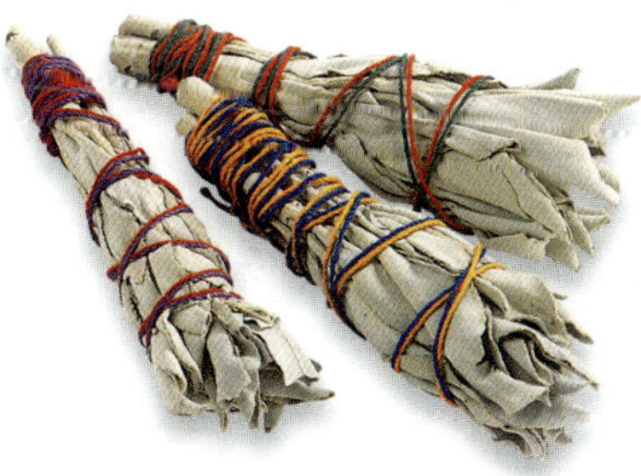

SELF-HEALING TREATMENTS

Whenever you are experiencing discomfort or are unwell, stressed, worried, emotionally upset, or just out of sorts, try giving yourself a crystal chakra self-healing treatment.

CRYSTAL SELF-HEALING

This self-healing treatment is also a good way of ending your day even if you feel well. Repeating this treatment daily will help to keep your energies in balance and maintain health. You can work with your crystal chakra set or, if there are specific issues or ailments you wish to treat, replace a standard chakra crystal with one of the others suggested in Chapter 4 or with one of the crystals that work on all the chakras (see pages 168–174).

Simply lie on your back in bed, on a sofa, or on the floor, and place the crystals in the appropriate position on your body (see page 53). Lie still and allow yourself to rest and relax for about half an hour. Play gentle, relaxing music and light some incense if you like.

The solar plexus chakra is depicted with bright sunshine yellow to symbolize energy.

AURA CLEANSING

This is a wonderful exercise to do at home after a hard day at work. It removes the "stuff" you've picked up in your aura during the day and aids the release of worrying thoughts and emotions. Stand with your feet apart in line with your shoulders, knees slightly bent, holding your quartz master crystal in your dominant hand. With the crystal pointing to the floor, move it slowly in a clockwise direction for five minutes. You will feel the weight coming off your shoulders as your crystal takes away anything you don't need. You will feel more centered within just a few minutes.

WEARING OR CARRYING CRYSTALS

Keeping crystals with you all the time is simple and effective. A good general balancing set is the crystal chakra set (see page 57), but each morning look at your collection and see if one wants to come out with you today.

Wearing crystal jewelry harnesses the healing qualities of your chosen stones.

DISTANT HEALING

Also known as remote or absent healing, distant healing involves projecting healing energy over a distance. Many crystal therapists like to include distant healing in their daily routine. You can work with your quartz master crystal, but some therapists prefer to have a special distant healing crystal. It might be ruby, tiger's eye, or quartz, but what it is doesn't matter, so long as it feels special to you.

An alternative method to the distant healing technique explained below is to sit quietly holding your quartz master crystal, with it pointing away from you, and focus your mind on a person, animal, or place in the world that might benefit from healing. Imagine a powerful white crystalline light emanating from the point of the crystal flowing to them. If your mind jumps from one person to another, just allow the light to flow to them.

You can work with crystals to send distant healing to a loved one far away.

PRACTICAL EXERCISE: Distant Healing

- When doing distant healing, you may like to play some soft, relaxing music, burn incense, dim the lights, and light a candle. Focus your intent on sending healing energies to the person you wish to heal. It may help you to focus on them if you hold a personal item of theirs. Write their name at the top of a piece of paper, and draw a picture of them that fills the page (a stick man or woman will do), or lay a full-length photograph of them on the paper beneath the name.
- Place your crystal chakra set over the chakras on the picture of the person.
- Take your quartz master crystal and move it clockwise over each crystal for about two minutes or until you feel a change (see page 188). This is much harder to sense than when you are working with someone who is in the same room. You can also ask God, spirit guides, angels, or whatever you believe is out there to help carry the crystal healing energy for you.

Spirit quartz and quartz crystal

GLOSSARY

Absent healing *See* **Distant healing**. The process of sending healing energy, good thoughts or prayers to a person who is not present—perhaps someone in another country. Also known as remote healing.

Aggregate A mixture of minerals combined in a geological process; it resembles a solid rock.

Akashic records A library of spiritual information that exists on another plane.

Alluvial Made from sediment in riverbeds which produces "river-tumbled" crystals.

Asterism An optical effect that results in a star-like appearance.

Astral travel The ability to send a part of the astral/spirit body to travel outside the physical body (while remaining connected to the physical body).

Aura The subtle energy field around the body.

Blade A crystal that resembles a flat knife blade.

Botryoidal Describes bulbous minerals that resemble a bunch of grapes.

Chakra The Sanskrit word for "wheel." Chakras are the energy centers of the body, appearing as wheels to people who see energy.

Chatoyancy An optical effect, also known as "cat's eye," found in some polished crystals. Chatoyant crystals bring good luck, happiness, and serenity. They raise intuition and awareness, provide protection, and can help with disorders of the eyes, night vision, and headaches. The astrological associations of these crystals are Capricorn, Taurus, and Aries.

Chi In Chinese medicine and philosophy, chi is the energy or life force of the universe, believed to flow around the body and to be present in all living things. Other cultures call chi by different names, such as prana in India.

Crust The top or outer layer. Crystals occurring as crusts are growing on the surface of a rock or mineral. *See also* **Druse**.

Crystal system A classification of crystals according to their atomic structure, describing them in terms of their axes (imaginary straight lines through the center, around which they are symmetrically arranged). The systems are hexagonal, isometric, monoclinic, orthorhombic, tetragonal, and triclinic.

Cubic Describes a cube-shaped crystal, with six square faces. The three axes are the same length and are at right angles to one another.

Dendrite A mineral that crystallizes in the shape of a tree or branch or grows through another crystal or rock, creating the impression of a tree or branches.

Dis-ease A state of unsoundness on any level (physical, emotional, mental, or spiritual), which may weaken the body's natural defense systems and increase the risk of illness or disease. It relates to underlying causes and not a specific illness or disease.

Distant healing The process of sending healing energy, good thoughts, or prayers to a person who is not present—perhaps someone in another country. Also known as absent healing or remote healing.

Dodecahedral Describes a crystal having 12 pentagonal (five-sided) faces meeting in threes at 20 vertexes.

Druse A surface crust of small crystals on a rock of the same or a different mineral.

Energy A supply or source of power: electrical, nuclear, mechanical, or subtle, e.g. chi.

Etheric Anything, on any level, linked to or by subtle energy.

Feldspar A group of silicate minerals.

Geode A hollow rock with crystals growing in the cavity.

Hexagonal Describes a crystal system having four axes, of which the three horizontal axes are equal in length and cross at 120° angles, and the vertical axis is a different length and at right angles to the others. A hexagonal crystal has eight faces.

Inclusion A mineral found within the structure of a different mineral.

Iridescence Colors appearing inside a crystal owing to either diffraction or refraction of light within the crystalline structure.

Isometric Describes a crystal system having three axes that are all equal in length and at right angles to one another.

Mass Matter that has no definable crystalline structure.

Meridian An energy pathway through the body. Meridians carry chi in the same way that veins and arteries carry blood.

Monoclinic Describes a crystal system having three unequal axes, only two of which are at right angles.

Nodule A form of a mineral that is massive (see **Mass**) with a rounded outer surface.

Octahedral Describes a crystal having eight faces that are all equilateral triangles; resembles two four-sided pyramids joined at the bases.

Orthorhombic Describes a crystal system having three axes of unequal lengths that cross at right angles.

Piezoelectric effect The electric current produced by some crystals when they are subjected to mechanical pressure.

Piezoelectricity The transducer effect that results from applying pressure to a crystal, allowing the transmutation of this mechanical energy into electrical energy. It creates a physical vibration which, in quartz crystal, resonates at a regular and constant frequency. This effect is very stable. So, if you have a quartz watch—and the quartz crystal is pure and cut at the correct angle to its axis—it will be accurate.

Plagioclase A series of feldspars, including labradorite and sunstone.

Plate A crystal that has grown flattened and often thin.

Prismatic Describes a crystal having faces that are similar in size and shape and that run parallel to an axis; the ends are rectilinear and similar in size and shape. For example, a triangular prismatic crystal has two triangular ends joined by three rectangular faces, while a hexagonal prismatic crystal has two hexagonal ends connected by sixrectangular faces.

Pseudomorph A mineral that replaces another within the original's crystal structure. As a result, the new mineral has the external shape of the departed one.

Psychic abilities These include intuition or gut feelings, channeling, clairaudience, clairsentience, clairvoyance, sensing energies and auras, seeing auras, interpreting auras, telepathy, extrasensory perception, and increased insight into divination and tarot card readings.

Pyramidal Describes a crystal in which the base is a polygon (i.e. with at least three straight sides) and the other faces are triangles that meet at a point.

Pyroelectric effect The production of electric charges on opposite faces of some crystals caused by a change in temperature.

Pyroelectricity The movement of electrons that results in a migration of positive and negative charges to opposite ends of a crystal. Caused by temperature changes, it is clearly seen in many crystals, especially tourmaline and quartz crystals. A weak effect can be observed in any crystal that has a polar axis.

Record keeper Describes a crystal with raised triangles on the face of the termination. Record keeper crystals help you access ancient wisdom and the Akashic records.

Reiki A form of hands-on healing that originated in Japan and now has millions of practitioners worldwide.

Remote healing *See* **Distant healing.**

Remote viewing The ability to see places and events at a distance. *See also* **Astral travel.**

Rhombohedral Describes a crystal which has six faces, each of them a rhombus (which has four equal sides, with opposite sides parallel, and no right angles). A rhombohedron resembles a cube that is skewed to one side.

Scalenohedral Describes crystals having 12 faces, each of them a scalene triangle (which has three unequal sides).

Shamanic healing An umbrella term covering a multitude of ancient forms of healing, all of which are linked to nature. It is one of the oldest forms of traditional healing.

Spirit guides The beings or energies of departed souls who impart knowledge and wisdom to help you on your path.

Striated Describes crystals having parallel grooves or markings along their length.

Subtle energy Energy that is outside of the known electromagnetic spectrum and therefore not easily detected.

Tabular Describes crystals that are broad and flat.

Tektite Small glassy rock formed from meteorite impact.

Tetragonal Describes a crystal system having three axes, of which only the two horizontal ones are equal, and all three axes are at right angles. It resembles a cube that has been stretched vertically.

Tetrahedral Describes crystals having four triangular faces.

Totem animals Animal spirits or characteristics that help to guide you on your path in life.

Trapezohedral Describes crystals having faces that each have four non-parallel sides (a shape known as a trapezium in the US and a trapezoid in the UK).

Triclinic Describes a crystal system having three axes, none of them equal in length or at right angles.

INDEX OF CRYSTALS

GENERAL INDEX

ACKNOWLEDGMENTS

I would like to thank my fabulous friend, Nicci Roscoe, for her unwavering support, for walking part of this journey we call life with me, and—most importantly—for making it fun.

A big thank you to all my students and clients, whose thoughtful questions have spurred the search for answers and helped bring this book to life. And, of course, the Stone People themselves, who are always willing helpers and active participants, providing stepping stones along the path.

To my wonderful team at The Crystal Healer Crystal Showroom—affectionately known as the Crystal Healer Helpers—Claire, Becky, and Rachel: thank you for all that you do.

Warm thanks to Liz Dean and Sonia Pugh for all their work and support on the first edition of this book, and to Carmel Edmonds for her thoughtful input into this pocket edition. I'd also like to mention Sally Powell, who always brings a touch of magic and beauty to the books we create, along with the rest of the dedicated team at CICO Books.

Thank you to Cindy Richards, for having faith in me at the very beginning, all those years ago, and to those who inspired me to write: my father, Cyril; the remarkable American crystal healer, Melody; and Ian, who knows why.

And finally, to everyone who feels inspired to heal themselves or others through the pages of this book—you are truly special.

ABOUT THE AUTHOR

Philip Permutt (www.thecrystalhealer.co.uk) is "Britain's leading crystal expert" (*Daily Mail*) and the author of many books, including *The Ancient Power of Crystals, Crystals for Everyday Living, Crystal Connections, The Modern Guide to Crystal Chakra Healing,* and the best-sellers *The Crystal Healer Volumes 1* and *2,* all published by CICO Books. Philip has been practicing as a crystal healer and teacher for almost 35 years. He owns a successful business importing and selling crystals and runs courses and workshops on working with crystals. He lives in Hertfordshire, UK.